T0256237

CHAPMAN & HALL/CRC THE PYTHON SERIES

About the Series

Python has been ranked as the most popular programming language, and it is widely used in education and industry. This book series will offer a wide range of books on Python for students and professionals. Titles in the series will help users learn the language at an introductory and advanced level, and explore its many applications in data science, AI, and machine learning. Series titles can also be supplemented with Jupyter notebooks.

Image Processing and Acquisition using Python, Second Edition
Ravishankar Chityala, Sridevi Pudipeddi

Python Packages
Tomas Beuzen and Tiffany-Anne Timbers

Statistics and Data Visualisation with Python
Jesús Rogel-Salazar

Introduction to Python for Humanists
William J.B. Mattingly

Python for Scientific Computation and Artificial Intelligence
Stephen Lynch

Learning Professional Python: Volume 1: The Basics
Usharani Bhimavarapu and Jude D. Hemanth

Learning Professional Python: Volume 2: Advanced
Usharani Bhimavarapu and Jude D. Hemanth

For more information about this series please visit: www.crcpress.com/ Chapman – HallCRC/book-series/PYTH

Learning Professional Python

Volume 2 of **Learning Professional Python** is a resource for students who want to learn Python even if they don't have any programming knowledge and for teachers who want a comprehensive introduction to Python to use with their students. This book helps the students achieve their dream job in the IT Industry and teaches the students in an easy, understandable manner while strengthening coding skills.

Learning Professional Python: Volume 2 Objectives

- Become familiar with the features of Python programming language

- Introduce the object-oriented programming concepts

- Discover how to write Python code by following the object-oriented programming concepts

- Become comfortable with concepts such as classes, objects, inheritance, dynamic dispatch, interfaces, and packages

- Learn the Python generics and collections

- Develop exception handling and the multithreaded applications

- Design graphical user interface (GUI) applications

Learning Professional Python

Python

Volume 2: Advanced

Usharani Bhimavarapu
and Jude D. Hemanth

CRC Press
Taylor & Francis Group
Boca Raton London New York

CRC Press is an imprint of the
Taylor & Francis Group, an **informa** business

A CHAPMAN & HALL BOOK

First edition published 2024
by CRC Press
2385 NW Executive Center Drive, Suite 320, Boca Raton FL 33431

and by CRC Press
4 Park Square, Milton Park, Abingdon, Oxon, OX14 4RN

CRC Press is an imprint of Taylor & Francis Group, LLC

© 2024 Usharani Bhimavarapu and Jude D. Hemanth

Library of Congress Cataloging-in-Publication Data
Names: Bhimavarapu, Usharani, author. | Hemanth, D. Jude, author.
Title: Learning professional Python / Usharani Bhimavarapu, D. Jude Hemanth.
Description: First edition. | Boca Raton : CRC Press, 2024. | Includes bibliographical references and index.
Identifiers: LCCN 2023007977 | ISBN 9781032539256 (volume 1 ; hbk) | ISBN 9781032534237 (volume 1 ; pbk) | ISBN 9781003414322 (volume 1 ; ebk) | ISBN 9781032611761 (volume 2 ; hbk) | ISBN 9781032611709 (volume 2 ; pbk) | ISBN 9781003462392 (volume 2 ; ebk)
Subjects: LCSH: Python (Computer program language) | Computer programming.
Classification: LCC QA76.73.P98 B485 2024 | DDC 005.13/3—dc23/eng/20230508
LC record available at https://lccn.loc.gov/2023007977

ISBN: 978-1-032-61176-1 (hbk)
ISBN: 978-1-032-61170-9 (pbk)
ISBN: 978-1-003-46239-2 (ebk)

DOI: 10.1201/9781003462392

Typeset in Minion
by Apex CoVantage, LLC

Contents

Preface

Python is a general-purpose interpreted programming language used for deep learning, machine learning, and complex data analysis. Python is a perfect language for beginners as it is easy to learn and understand. This book is intended to teach the reader how to program in Python. The book aims to get you up to speed fast enough and have you writing real Python programs in no time at all. It assumes no previous exposure to the Python language and is suited to both beginners and experienced programmers. This book gives a comprehensive, in-depth introduction to the core Python language.

This book helps you in gaining a quick grasp of the fundamentals of Python programming and working with built-in functions. The book then moves to help you in exception handling, data wrangling, databases with Python, regular expressions, NumPy arrays, data frames and plotting. The Python Programming culminates with how you can continue learning Python after reading this book and leaves you with a problem to solve, testing your skills even at the last step.

The book contains approximately 500 tested programs, and all these programs have been tested using the IDE Anaconda, Google colaboratory, and Python online compilers compatible to the Windows operating system and discussed the appropriate nature of the output. The book further mentions a summary of the technical aspects of interviewing tips on negotiating the best offer and guiding the best way.

This book is for data analysts, IT developers, and anyone looking to get started with or transition to the field of software or refresh their knowledge of Python programming. This book will also be useful for students planning to build a career in data engineering or IT professionals preparing for a transition. No previous knowledge of data engineering is required. The book aims to get you up to speed fast enough and have you writing real Python programs in no time at all.

It contains 10 chapters, with practice exercises given at the end of the first nine chapters to enable the learners to review the knowledge gained. Each chapter starts with a brief introduction, top tips, and a review of the essential library methods, finally followed by broad and thought-provoking problems.

We are thankful to Taylor and Francis Publications for undertaking the publication of this book and supporting us in this endeavor. Any suggestions for the improvement of the book will be thankfully acknowledged and incorporated in the next edition.

Dr. Usharani Bhimavarapu
Dr. Jude D. Hemanth

Author Biographies

Usharani Bhimavarapu is working as an assistant professor in the Computer Science and Engineering Department at Koneru Lakshmaiah Education Foundation at Vaddeswaram, Andhra Pradesh, India. She has been teaching for the last 14 years with emphasis on data mining, machine learning, and data structure. She communicated more than 40 research papers in SCI, SCIE, and Scopus indexed journals. She has authored 12 books in programming languages like CPP, Java, Python, HTML, CSS, and so on.

Dr. Jude D. Hemanth received his BE degree in ECE from Bharathiar University in 2002, ME degree in communication systems from Anna University in 2006, and PhD from Karunya University in 2013. His research areas include computational intelligence and image processing. He has authored more than 230 research papers in reputed SCIE indexed international journals and Scopus indexed international conferences. His cumulative impact factor is more than 350. He has published 37 edited books with reputed publishers such as Elsevier, Springer, and IET.

He has been serving as an associate editor of SCIE indexed international journals such as *IEEE Journal of Biomedical and Health Informatics* (IEEE-JBHI), *IEEE Transactions on Intelligent Transportation Systems*, *Soft Computing* (Springer), *Earth Science Informatics* (Springer), *IET Image Processing*, *Heliyon* (Elsevier), *Mathematical Problems in Engineering*, *PeerJ Computer Science*, *PLOS One*, and *Dyna* (Spain). He also holds the associate editor/guest editor position with many Scopus journals. He has been serving as the series editor of Biomedical Engineering series (Elsevier), editorial board member of ASTI series (Springer), and Robotics and Healthcare series (CRC Press).

He has received a project grant of 35,000 UK pounds from the UK government (GCRF scheme) with collaborators from the University of Westminster, UK. He has also completed two funded research projects from CSIR and DST, the government of India. He also serves as the research scientist of Computational Intelligence and Information Systems (CI2S) Lab, Argentina; LAPISCO Research Lab, Brazil; RIADI Lab, Tunisia; Research Centre for Applied Intelligence, University of Craiova, Romania; and eHealth and Telemedicine Group, University of Valladolid, Spain.

He is the NVIDIA university ambassador and NVIDIA certified instructor for deep learning courses. His name was featured in the "Top 2% Leading World Scientists" [2021, 2022] list released by Stanford University, USA. He is an international accreditation member for higher education institutions in Romania [ARACIS] and Slovenia [SQAA] under the European Commission. Currently, he is working as a professor in the Department of ECE, Karunya University, Coimbatore, India.

## CHAPTER 1

Classes and Objects

1.1 CREATING CLASSES

The class keyword generates a new class definition. The name of the class instantly follows the keyword class followed by a colon. The class definition starts with the keyword class. The keyword is followed by a user-defined class name followed by a colon (:). The code inside the block defines all the class variable and class functions. The pass keyword fills the class with nothing, it does not contain any methods and variables.

Syntax

```
Class class-name:
Class members
Class attributes
Class functions
```

Example

```
class test:
val=10
def display(self):
print("val=",val)
```

The variable Val is the class variable whose value is allocated among all the instances of that specified class. Class methods is different from that of the normal functions, the first argument of the class methods is the self-argument. Python automatically adds up the self-argument to the

DOI: 10.1201/9781003462392-1

methods, the programmers need not include the self-argument at the time of calling the methods.

1.1.1 Python Self-Parameter

The self-parameter describes the current instance of the class and access the class variables. The self must be the first parameter of the class-related functions.

1.2 OBJECT CREATION

Creating an object to the class is called instantiation.

Syntax

```
Object-name= class-name([arguments])
For example
t=test ()
```

The different objects of the same class may consist of different properties. Each object has their own set of data i.e., no objects interfere with each other. The class method may be invoked without an argument but not declared without parameters. The first parameter of all the class methods must be the self-parameter. There is no need to pass the argument for the self-parameter. Python will automatically the argument for the self-parameter. If the programmer wants to accept the parameters other than self, they should be placed after the self in the class method definition. The self-parameter is used to obtain access to the objects instance and the class variables. The self-parameter is used to invoke the other class methods from inside the class.

Note: By modifying the one class data does not affect the remaining class objects.

Program

```
Class test:
def_new_(cls):
print("creating object")
def_init_(self):
print("initialisation")
```

```
test()
t=test()
```

Output

```
creating object
creating object
```

The preceding program is for __new__ method. __new__ method returns the instance of the class.

Program

```
class test:
def _new_(cls):
print("creating object")
return super(test,cls)._new_(cls)
def _init_(self):
print("initialisation")
test()
```

Output

```
creating object
initialisation
<__main__.test at 0x7f113652b790>
```

Program

```
i="outside class"
class test:
i="inside class"
def display(self):
i="inside method"
print("inside display method:",i)
def put(self):
print("inside put method:",i)
t=test()
t.display()
t.put()
print(i)
print("class variable from outside class:",t.i)
```

Output

```
inside display method: inside method
inside put method: outside class
outside class
class variable from outside class: inside class
```

The preceding program is about the creating a variable to the class outside the class.

1.3 ACCESSING ATTRIBUTES

To invoke the methods or variables of the class, use the dot notation. The programmers can retrieve the objects attributes using the dot operator with object. Class variables can be retrieved using class name, then a dot(.) operator after the object and specify the desired properties (i.e., variables or methods). When the class components start with two underscores (__), means it is private component. The objects of the same class do not contain the same data.

Syntax for class variables

```
Object-name. class-variable-name
```

Syntax for calling class methods

```
Object-name. class-method-name([arguments])
For example
To access test class variable Val
test.val
to invoke the class methods
t.display()
```

Now combine all code into one part.

```
class test:
val=10
def display(self):
print("val=",val)
t=test()
print(test.val)
t.display()
```

The programmers can enhance, delete, or alter attributes of classes and objects at any time.

```
t.i=100
t.i=50
del t.i
```

The programmers can define the variables outside the class, inside the class, and inside the method also (Table 1.1).

TABLE 1.1   Variables and its accessibility scope

Variables Defined and Initialized In	Outside class	Inside class	Inside method
Outside class	Yes	Yes	Yes
Inside class	No	Yes	Yes
Inside method	No	Yes	Yes

1.4 CLASS METHOD

A class method in Python is a method that is bound to the class but not to the instance.

Python consists of decorators @classmethod, @staticmethod.

The class methods can be created in Python by two ways.

1. By using the factory method class method ()

2. By using the @classmethod decorator

The factory method class method () is bound to a class rather than an object. The class methods can be called by both class and object.

Syntax for factory class method

```
class-name. function-name=class-method(class-name.
  function-name)
class-name.function-name()
The @classmethod decorator is a built in function
  decorator receives the class as the implicit first
argument, especially cls. cls represents the class
  that is instantiated.
syntax for classmethod decorator
@classmethod
def function-name(cls, args, . . .)
```

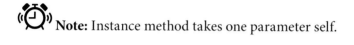 **Note:** Instance method takes one parameter self.

Program

```
class test:
def display(self):
print("istance method")
@classmethod
def put(cls):
print("class method")
@staticmethod
def function():
print("static method")
t=test()
t.display()
test.put()
test.function()
```

Output

```
istance method
class method
static method
```

The preceding program shows how to access the instance method, class method, and static method.

Class method syntax

```
@classmethod
def functionname(cls,args . . ..):
#class function body
```

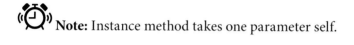 **Note:** class methods take the parameter cls and a decorator @ classmethod.

Example

```
class test:
@classmethod
def put(cls):
print("class method")
test.put()
```

Output

```
class method
```

Invocation of class method

```
classname.classmethodname()
e.g.: test.put() #put is the class method in the class
  test
```

Static method inside class syntax

```
class classname:
@staticmethod
def functionname():
#static method body
```

Static method invocation

```
classname.staticmethodname()
```

Example

```
class test:
@staticmethod
def function():
print("static method")
test.function()
```

Output

```
static method
```

Program

```
class test:
i=1
f=1.1
s="python"
@classmethod
def put(cls):
print(cls.i)
print(cls.f)
print(cls.s)
test.put()
```

Output

```
1
1.1
python
```

The preceding program using class variables and display using class method.

Program

```
class test:
@classmethod
def put(cls,i,f,s):
print(i)
print(f)
print(s)
test.put(1,1.1, "python")
```

Output

```
1
1.1
Python
```

The preceding program invokes class method with parameters.

Program

```
class test:
i=10
f=1.10
s="pyhton"
def put(obj):
print(obj.i)
print(obj.f)
print(obj.s)
test.put=classmethod(test.put)
test.put()
```

Output

```
10
1.1
pyhton
```

The preceding program used class method without using decorator@ classmethod and by using factory method classmethod().

Program

```
class test:
def __init__ (self,i,j):
self.i=i
self.j=j
def display(self):
print("i=",self.i,"j=",self.j)
t1=test(10,1.1)
t2=test("python","test")
t3=test(50,"python")
print("t1 object")
t1.display()
print("t2 object")
t2.display()
print("t3 object")
t3.display()
```

Output

```
t1 object
i= 10 j= 1.1
t2 object
i= python j= test
t3 object
i= 50 j= python
```

The preceding program demonstrates the managing class variables.

Program: Try except when invalid class variables are invoked (place this example in exception handling chapter)

```
      class test:
class test:
def __init__(self,i,j):
self.i=i
self.j=j
def display(self):
print("i=",self.i,"j=",self.j)
```

```
t1=test(10,1.1)
try:
print(t1.i)
print(t1.k)
except Exception as e:
print(e.__class__)
```

Output

```
10
<class 'AttributeError'>
```

Program

```
class test:
def __init__(self):
print("constructor")
def put(self):
print("invoked from class method")
def display(this_object):
print("class method")
this_object.put()
t1=test()
t1.display()
```

Output

```
constructor
class method
invoked from class method
```

The preceding program invokes class method using self-inside the class.

Program

```
class test:
pass
t1=test()
```

Output: No output

The preceding uses the pass statement in class creation

Program

```
class test (object):
def f1(self):
pass

def f2(self):
print("function-2")
t=test()
t.f1()
t.f2()
```

Output

```
function-2
```

The preceding program used the pass statement for the class methods.

Program

```
class test(object):
def __iter__(self):
x = 1
yield x
yield x + 1
yield x + 2

t= test()
for i in t:

print(i)
for i in t:

print(i)
```

Output

```
1
2
3
1
2
3
```

The preceding program used the yield statement.

Program

```
class test:
def display():
print("static method")
test.display=staticmethod(test.display)
test.display()
```

Output

```
static method
```

The preceding program used the static method without parameters.

Program

```
class test:
def display(i,f,s):
print(i)
print(f)
print(s)
test.display=staticmethod(test.display)
test.display(10,10.123, "python")
```

Output

```
10
10.123
python
```

The preceding program used the static method factory method with parameters.

Program

```
class test:
@staticmethod
def display(i,f,s):
print(i)
print(f)
print(s)
test.display(10,10.123, "python")
```

Output

```
10
10.123
python
```

The preceding program used the static method decorator method with parameters.

1.5 RETURN FROM CLASS

The class methods use the cls parameter instead of the self parameter.

Program

```
from datetime import date
class test:
def __init__(self, name, age):
self.name = name
self.age = age

@classmethod
def dob(cls, name, y):
return cls(name, date.today().year - y)

def display(self):
print(self.name + "'s age is: " + str(self.age))
t = test('usha', 34)
t.display()

t1 = test.dob('rani', 1987)
t1.display()
```

Output

```
usha's age is: 34
rani's age is: 34
```

The preceding program returns class method using cls.

Program

```
class test:
def __init__(self,i,s):
```

```
self.i=i
self.s=s
@classmethod
def put(cls,i,s):
i=10+i
s="new "+s
return cls(i,s)
def display(self):
print(self.i)
print(self.s)
t=test.put(10,"python")
t.display()
```

Output

```
20
new python
```

The preceding program returns cls object using factory method class method.

1.6 CONSTRUCTORS

A constructor is a Python function that is employed to set the instance members of the class.

In Python, the function __init__ () is used for the constructor of the class. The constructor is called when the class is instantiated, and it takes the self-keyword as the first parameter, which is applied to access the attributes or methods of the class. Every class in the Python has the default constructor when the programmer does not provide the explicit constructor. The constructor is of three types:

1. Default constructor

2. Parameter-less constructor

3. Parameterized constructor

Program

```
class test:
def display(self):
print("display method")
```

```
t=test()
t.display()
```

Output

```
display method
```

The preceding program uses the default constructor.

Program

```
class test:
def __init__(self):
print("parameter less constructor")
def display(self):
print("display method")
t=test()
t.display()
```

Output

```
parameter less constructor
display method
```

The preceding program used the parameter-less constructor.

Program

```
class test
def __init__(self,s=None):
print("parameterized constructor")
t1=test("python")
```

Output

```
parameterized constructor
```

The preceding program used the parameterized constructor.

Program

```
class test:
c=0
def __init__(self):
```

```
test.c+=1
t=test()
t1=test()
t2=test()
print(test.c)
```

Output

3

The preceding program used the count the number of objects in the class.

Program

```
class test:
def __init__(self):
print("constructor-1")
def __init__(self):
print("constructor-2 ")
test()
```

Output

```
constructor-2
<__main__.test at 0x7f11364a0b10>
```

The preceding program is for constructor overloading with two constructors.

Program: Constructor overloading

```
class test:
def __init__(self):
print("One")
def __init__(self):
print("Two")
def __init__(self):
print("Three")
t = test()
```

Output

Three

The preceding program is for constructor overloading with three constructors.

A constructor can be invoked automatically when the object of the class is instantiated. If a class has a constructor, then it is invoked automatically.

1. The constructor's name in Python is always __init__.

2. In Python, the constructor has at least one parameter, that is, self.

3. Constructor does not return values.

4. Constructors cannot be invoked manually either from the object or from inside the class. Constructors are invoked automatically.

Program: Constructor

Note: There is the need to place the self-argument at the arguments list to only class methods and constructors.

1.7 DELETING OBJECTS

Python removes surplus objects inevitably to set free the memory space. The process by which Python continually recovers blocks of memory that no longer are in usage is called as garbage collection. Python garbage collector operates during program execution and is activated when an objects reference count gets zero. An objects reference count modifications as the number of aliases that point to its shifts. An objects reference count raises when it is allocated a new name or arranged in another type. The object reference count reduces when it's removed using del. When reference is shifted, it is reassigned or its reference goes out of scope. The programmer does not observe when the garbage collector extinguishes the unused object and recovers its space. The programmer invokes the destructor __del__ () to destroy the object and reclaims the memory space. This method cleans up the non-used memory resources utilized by the instance.

Program

```
class test:
def __init__(self):
print('Object created.')
def __del__(self):
```

```
print('Destructor called, Object deleted.')
t = test()
del t
```

Output

```
Object created.
Destructor called, Object deleted.
```

The preceding program used the destructor.

1.7.1 Delete the Object

The programmer can delete the object itself by using the del keyword.

Program

```
class test:
i=10
def display(self):
print("i=",self.i)
t=test()
t.display()
del t
```

Output

```
i= 10
```

The preceding program deleted the class object using the del keyword.

Program

```
class test:
i=10
j=20
st="python"
def display(self):
print("i=",self.i,"j=",self.j,
"String=",self.st)
t=test()
t.display()
#del t.i
delattr(test, 'i')
```

Output

```
i= 10 j= 20 String= python
```

The preceding program deleted the class object properties.

If we call t.display() method after deleting the class attribute, then an error will occur.

```
class test:
i=10
j=20
st="python"
def display(self):
print("i=",self.i,"j=",self.j,
"String=",self.st)
t=test()
t.display()
delattr(test, 'i')
t.display()
```

Output

```
i= 10 j= 20 String= python
-----------------------------------------------------------------
AttributeError         Traceback (most recent call last)
<ipython-input-1-1f8d0b195e51> in <module>()
10 #del t.i
11 delattr(test, 'i')
---> 12 t.display()

<ipython-input-1-1f8d0b195e51> in display(self)
4                  st="python"
5                  def display(self):
----> 6
           print("i=",self.i,"j=",self.j,
7                      "String=",self.st)
8 t=test()
AttributeError: 'test' object has no attribute 'i'
```

Program

```
class test:
s1 = "this"
```

```
s2 = "is"
s3 = "to"
s4 = "test"
s5 = "delete"

t = test()

print('test before delattr()--')
print('First = ',t.s1)
print('Second = ',t.s2)
print('Third = ',t.s3)
print('Fourth = ',t.s4)
print('Fifth = ',t.s5)

delattr(test, 's5')
print('After deleting fifth attribute--')
print('First = ',t.s1)
print('Second = ',t.s2)
print('Third = ',t.s3)
print('Fourth = ',t.s4)
# this statement raises an error
print('Fifth = ',t.s5)

test before delattr()--
First = this
Second = is
Third = to
Fourth = test
Fifth = delete
After deleting fifth attribute--
First = this
Second = is
Third = to
Fourth = test
```

Before at
```
----------------------------------------------------------
AttributeError                         Traceback (most
recent call last)
<ipython-input-110-e423d99f8079> in <module>()
25 print('Fourth = ',t.s4)
```

```
26 # this statement raises an error
---> 27 print('Fifth = ',t.s5)

AttributeError: 'test' object has no attribute 's5'
```

The preceding program demonstrated the deleting of the attributes.

1.8 PYTHON BUILT-IN CLASS FUNCTIONS

The predefined built functions of the Python are tabulated in Table 1.2.

TABLE 1.2 Predefined Class Functions

Function	Description
getattr(obj, name, default)	Used to access the attribute of the object
setattr(obj,name, value)	Used to set a particular value to the specific attribute of the object
delattr(obj,name)	Used to delete a specific attribute
hasattr (obj,name)	Returns true if the object contains the specific attribute

Program

```
class test:
def __init__(self):
print()
def getattribute(self):
return self.a,self.b
def setattribute(self,a,b):
self.a=a
self.b=b

t=test()
t.setattribute(10,100)
print(t.getattribute())
```

Output

```
(10, 100)
```

The preceding program used the getattr and the setattr.

Program

```
class test:
def __init__(self):
self.a=0
self.b=0
def getattribute(self):
return self.a,self.b
def setattribute(self,a,b):
self.a=a
self.b=b

t=test()
t.setattribute(10,100)
print(t.getattribute())
delattr(t,'a')
print(t.b)
```

Output

```
(10, 100)
100
```

The preceding program used delattr method to delete the attributes.

Program

```
class test:
def __init__(self):
self.a=0
self.b=0
def getattribute(self):
return self.a,self.b
def setattribute(self,a,b):
self.a=a
self.b=b

t=test()
t.setattribute(10,100)
print(t.getattribute())
delattr(t,'a')
print(hasattr(t.'a'))
print(hasattr(t.'b'))
```

Output

```
(10, 100)
False
True
```

The preceding program used hasattr.

1.9 BUILT-IN CLASS ATTRIBUTES

Python predefined attributes are tabulated in Table 1.3.

TABLE 1.3   Built-In Class Attributes

Attribute	Description
__dict__	Contains the class namespaces
__doc__	Class documentation
__name__	Class name
__module__	Module name in which class is defined
__bases__	Tuple containing the base classes of their occurrence

Program

```
class test:
c = 0
def __init__(self, s, sal):
self.s= s
self.sal = sal
test.c += 1
def dcount(self):
print(" #:objects %d" % test.c)
def display(self):
print("Name : ", self.salary, ", Salary: ", self.sal)

print ("test.__doc__:", test.__doc__)
print ("test.__name__:", test.__name__)
print ("test.__module__:", test.__module__)
print ("test.__bases__:", test.__bases__)
print ("test.__dict__:", test.__dict__)
```

Output

```
test.__doc__: None
test.__name__: test
test.__module__: __main__
test.__bases__: (<class 'object'>,)

test.__dict__: {'__module__': '__main__', 'c': 0,
   '__init__': <function test.__init__ at
   0x7fc76c755f80>, 'dcount': <function test.dcount at
   0x7fc76c755950>, 'display': <function test.display
   at 0x7fc76c755c20>, '__dict__': <attribute '__
   dict__' of 'test' objects>,'__
   weakref__':<attribute'__weakref__'of 'test'
   objects>,'__doc__': None}
```

The preceding program used the built-in class attributes.

1.10 INNER CLASS

A class defined in another class is known as inner class, or nested class. If an object is built using inner class, then the object can also be employed by parent class. A parent class can have one or more inner class.

Advantage: Hide the code.

There are two types of inner class in Python.

1. Multilevel inner class – The class comprises inner class and again this inner class comprises another inner class.

2. Multiple inner class – Class includes one or more inner classes.

Program

```
class outer:
s="outer"
def __init__(self):
self.inn=self.inner()
print("outer class constructor")
class inner:
def __init__(self):
print("inner class constructor")
o=outer()
i=o.inn
```

Output

```
inner class constructor
outer class constructor
```

The preceding program is *invoking inner class constructor.*

Program

```
class outer:
def _init_(self):
self.inn=self.inner()
self.inn.nes=self.inner.nested()
print("outer class constructor")
class inner:
def _init_(self):
print("inner class constructor")
class nested:
def _init_(self):
print("nested class constructor")

o=outer()
i=o.inn
n=o.inn.nes
```

Output

```
inner class constructor
nested class constructor
outer class constructor
```

The preceding program created the nested class called nested in the inner class.

Program

```
class outer:
s="outer"
def _init_(self):
self.inn1=self.inner1()
self.inn2=self.inner2()
self.inn3=self.inner3()
print("outer class constructor")
```

```
class inner1:
def _init_(self):
print("first inner class constructor")
class inner2:
def _init_(self):
print("second inner class constructor")
class inner3:
def _init_(self):
print("third inner class constructor")
o=outer()
i1=o.inn1
i2=o.inn2
i3=o.inn3
```

Output

```
first inner class constructor
second inner class constructor
third inner class constructor
outer class constructor
```

The preceding program created more than one inner classes in the single outer class.

EXERCISE

1. Print the instance name of the class.

2. Construct the class named circle and find the area and the perimeter of the circle.

3. Construct the class named rectangle and compute the area of the rectangle.

4. Construct the class named string and print the string in the uppercase.

5. Construct the class student and print the grade of the student.

6. Create the inner class named age in the outer class named student and find the age of the student as per today's date.

## CHAPTER 2

Inheritance

A child class can override data members and methods from the parent class. The child class gets the properties and can retrieve all the data properties and functions specified in the parent class. A child class can support their own implementations along with the parent class implementations. The main advantage of the inheritance is the code reusability.

The different types of inheritance are as follows:

1. Single inheritance

2. Multiple inheritance

3. Multilevel inheritance

2.1 SINGLE INHERITANCE

A single child class is derived from a single parent class. The representation of the single inheritance is illustrated in Figure 2.1.

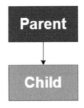

FIGURE 2.1 Single inheritance.

DOI: 10.1201/9781003462392-2

Syntax

```
class childclassname({parent-1)
```

In Python, a child class inherits base class by declaring the base in the bracket following the child class name.

Program

```
class Parent:
def func1(self):
print("this is parent")
class Child(Parent):
def func2(self):
print("this is child")

ob = Child()
ob.func1()
ob.func2()
```

Output

```
this is parent
this is child
```

In the preceding program, Parent is the parent class name, whereas the Child is the child class name. Child class used the single inheritance concept, so it acquires all the parent class properties. The object ob is instantiated for the child class because of inheritance. The ob object calls the parent class function func1.

2.2 MULTIPLE INHERITANCE

In Python a class can inherit many classes by declaring all base class within the bracket (Figure 2.2).

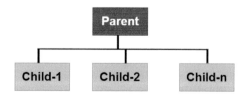

FIGURE 2.2 Multiple inheritance.

Syntax

```
class base1:
[class properties and members]
class base2:
[class properties and members]
. . . . . . . . . . . . .. . . . . . . . . .
class baseN:
[class properties and members]
class childclass(base1,base2, . . . . .)
[class properties and members]
```

Program

```
# Base class
class base:
# Constructor
def __init__(self, name):
self.name = name
# To get name
def getName(self):
return self.name
# To check if this person is employee
def isemployee(self):
return "is not a employee"
# Derived class
class derived(base):
# True is returned
def isemployee(self):
return "is a employee"

b = base("usha")
print(b.getName(), b.isemployee())

d = derived("rani")
print(d.getName(), d.isemployee())
```

Output

```
usha is not a employee
rani is a employee
```

2.3 MULTILEVEL INHERITANCE

Multilevel inheritance is deriving a child class not directly from the base class, that is, child class is derived from another derived class (Figure 2.3).

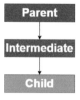

FIGURE 2.3   Multilevel inheritance.

Syntax

```
class base:
[class properties and members]
class child1(base):
[class properties and members]
class child2(child1):
[class properties and members]
```

Child2 is deriving not directly from the direct base class instead deriving from the child1, which is derived from the base class.

Program

```
# Base class
class base:
def __init__(self, name):
self.name = name

# Intermediate class
class derived(base):
def __init__(self, s, name):
self.s = s
base.__init__(self, name)

# Derived class
class subderived(derived):
def __init__(self,s1, s, name):
self.s1 = s1
```

```
# invoking constructor of derived class
derived.__init__(self, s, name)

def display(self):
print('base name :', self.name)
print("derived name :", self.s)
print("sub derived name :", self.s1)

ob = subderived('Bhimavarapu', 'usha', 'rani')
print(ob.name)
ob.display()
```

Output

```
rani
base name : rani
derived name : usha
sub derived name : Bhimavarapu
```

2.4 OVERRIDING METHODS

When the parent class method is (re)defined in the child class with a few modifications, then it is method overriding (Table 2.1).

TABLE 2.1 Python Base Overloading Methods

Methods	Description
__init__(self[,args . . .])	constructor
__del__(self)	destructor
__repr__(self)	String representation
__str__(self)	print string
__cmp__(self,x)	comparison

Program

```
class test:
@classmethod
def put(cls):
print("parent class method")
class sample(test):
pass
sample.put()
```

Output

```
parent class method
```

The preceding program invokes parent class method using the child class.

Program

```
class test:
@classmethod
def put(cls):
print("parent class method")
class sample(test):
@classmethod
def put(cls):
print("child class method")
sample.put()
```

Output

```
child class method
```

The preceding program overriding parent class method.

Program

```
class test:
@classmethod
def put(cls):
print("parent class method")
class sample(test):
@classmethod
def put(cls):
super().put()
print("child class method")
sample.put()
```

Output

```
parent class method
child class method
```

The preceding program overriding parent class methods using super ().

Program

```
Class test:
@classmethod
def put(cls):
print("parent class method")
class sample(test):
@classmethod
def put(cls):
test.put()
print("child class method")
sample.put()
```

Output

```
parent class method
child class method
```

The preceding program overriding parent class, class method.

Program

```
class test:
def put(self):
print("parent class method")
class sample(test):
def put(self):
super().put()
print("child class method")
s=sample()
s.put()
```

Output

```
parent class method
child class method
```

The preceding program overriding parent class instance method.

Program

```
class test:
def put(self):
print("parent class method")
```

```
class sample(test):
def put(self):
test.put(self)
print("child class method")
s=sample()
s.put()
```

Output

```
parent class method
child class method
```

The preceding program overriding parent class instance method using parentclassname.method(self).

Program

```
class base:
def __init__(self, s):
self.s = s
class derived(base):
def __init__(self, s, n):
base.__init__(self, s)
self.n = n
d = derived("python", 10)
print(d.s)
print(d.n)
```

Output

```
python
10
```

The preceding program invoking the parent class constructor from the child class.

Program

```
class A:
def __init__(self, txt):
print(txt,'A Class')
class B(A):
def __init__(self, txt):
```

```
print(txt,' B class')
super().__init__(txt)
class C(B):
def __init__(self, txt):
print(txt,' C class')
super().__init__(txt)
class D(B):
def __init__(self, txt):
print(txt,' D class')
super().__init__(txt)
class E(D, C):
def __init__(self):
print (' E class')
super().__init__('testing ')
d = E()
h = C('python')
```

Output

```
E class
testing      D class
testing     C class
testing    B class
testing   A Class
python   C class
python  B class
python  A Class
```

The preceding program invoking the parent class constructor from the child class using super.

Program

```
class base:
def show(self):
print("Inside base class")
class derived(base):
def display(self):
super().show()
print("Inside derived class")
d = derived()
d.display()
d.show()
```

Output

```
Inside base class
Inside derived class
```

The preceding program invoking the parent class method.

Program

```
# Defining parent class
class base():
# Constructor
def __init__(self):
self.value = "Inside Parent"
# Parent's show method
def show(self):
print(self.value)
# Defining child class
class derived(base):
# Constructor
def __init__(self):
self.value = "Inside Child"
# Child's show method
def show(self):
print(self.value)
ob1 = base()
ob2 = derived()
ob1.show()
ob2.show()
```

Output

```
Inside Parent
Inside Child
```

The preceding program overrides the parent class method.

Program

```
class test:
@classmethod
def put(cls,i,f,s):
print(i)
print(f)
```

```
print(s)
class sample(test):
pass
sample.put(1,1.1,"python")
```

Output

```
1
1.1
python
```

The preceding program used @classmethod for inheritance.

Program

```
class test:
@staticmethod
def put(i,f,s):
print(i)
print(f)
print(s)
class sample(test):
pass
sample.put(1,1.1,"python")
```

Output

```
1
1.1
python
```

The preceding program used @static method for inheritance with parameters.

Program

```
class test:
def display():
print("static method")
class sample(test):
pass
sample.display=staticmethod(sample.display)
sample.display()
```

Output

```
static method
```

The preceding program used static factory method inheritance.

Program

```
class test:
def display(i,f,s):
print(i)
print(f)
print(s)
class sample(test):
pass
sample.display=staticmethod(sample.display)
sample.display(10,10.123,"python")
```

Output

```
10
10.123
python
```

The preceding program used static factory method inheritance with parameters.

Program

```
class test:
@staticmethod
def display():
print("static decorator")
class sample(test):
pass
sample.display()
```

Output

```
static decorator
```

The preceding program used @static method for inheritance without parameters.

Program

```
class test:
def __new__(cls):
print("parent creating object")
def __init__(self):
print("parent initialisation")
class sample(test):
pass
sample()
```

Output

```
parent creating object
```

The preceding program used the constructor and the new method for the parent class and anonymous object creation for the child class.

Program

```
class test:
def __new__(cls):
print("parent creating object")
def __init__(self):
print("parent initialisation")
class sample(test):
def __new__(cls):
print("child creating object")
def __init__(self):
print("child initialisation")
sample()
```

Output

```
child creating object
```

The preceding program used the constructor and the new method for both the parent and the child classes and anonymous object creation for the child class.

Program

```
class test:
def __new__(cls):
```

```
print("parent creating object")
def __init__(self):
print("parent initialisation")
class sample(test):
def __new__(cls):
print("child creating object")
return test()
def __init__(self):
print("child initialisation")
sample()
```

Output

```
child creating object
parent creating object
```

The preceding program used the return test() in the child class new method. It invokes the parent class new method.

Program

```
class test:
def __new__(cls):
print("parent creating object")

def __init__(self):
print("parent initialisation")
class sample(test):
def __new__(cls):
super().__new__(cls)
print("child creating object")

def __init__(self):
print("child initialisation")
sample()
```

Output

```
parent creating object
child creating object
```

The preceding program invokes the super class new method using the super().

Program

```
class test:
def __init__(self):
print("parent initialisation")
class sample(test):
def __init__(self):
super().__init__()
print("child initialisation")
sample()
```

Output

```
parent initialisation
child initialisation
<__main__.sample at 0x7fc76c815ed0>
```

In the preceding program the parent class constructor was invoked from the child class by using the super ().

Program

```
class test:
def __init__(self):
print("parent zero-parameter initialisation")
def __init__(self,s):
print("parent one-parameter initialisation")
class sample(test):
def __init__(self):
super().__init__()
print("child zero-parameter initialisation")
def __init__(self,s):
super().__init__(s)
print("child one-parameter initialisation")
sample("python")
```

Output

```
parent one-parameter initialisation
child one-parameter initialisation
<__main__.sample at 0x7fc76c7f3d50>
```

In the preceding program the parent class parameterized constructor was invoked from the child class by using the super ().

2.5 NESTED CLASS INHERITANCE

The inheritance can be applied to the inner class, nested class, and also the multiple inner class.

Program

```
class outer:
def __init__(self):
self.inn=self.inner()
self.inn.nes=self.inner.nested()
print("outer class constructor")
class inner:
def __init__(self):
print("inner class constructor")
class nested:
def __init__(self):
print("nested class constructor")'

class multi(outer):
def __init__(self):
super().__init__()
print("child constructor")
o=multi()
i=o.inn
n=o.inn.nes
```

Output

```
inner class constructor
nested class constructor
outer class constructor
child constructor
```

The preceding program is about nested class, and inheritance maintains the inner class for the parent class and the normal child class.

Program

```
class outer:
def __init__(self):
self.inn=self.inner()
self.inn.nes=self.inner.nested()
```

```
print("outer class constructor")
class inner:
def __init__(self):

print("inner class constructor")
class nested:
def __init__(self):
print("nested class constructor")

class multi(outer):
def __init__(self):
super().__init__()
self.childinn=self.multiinner()
self.inn.childnes=self.multiinner.multinested()
print("child constructor")
class multiinner:
def __init__(self):
print("child inner class constructor")
class multinested:
def __init__(self):
print("child nested class constructor")
o=multi()
i=o.childinn
n=i.multinested
```

Output

```
inner class constructor
nested class constructor
outer class constructor
child inner class constructor
child nested class constructor
child constructor
```

The preceding program maintains the inner class for both the parent class and the child class.

Program

```
class outer:
def __init__(self):
self.inn1=self.inner1()
self.inn2=self.inner2()
```

```
self.inn3=self.inner3()
print("outer class constructor")
class inner1:
def __init__(self):
print("first inner class constructor")
class inner2:
def __init__(self):
print("second inner class constructor")
class inner3:
def __init__(self):
print("third inner class constructor")

class multi(outer):
def __init__(self):
super().__init__()
print("child constructor")
o=multi()
i1=o.inn1
i2=o.inn2
i3=o.inn3
```

Output

```
first inner class constructor
second inner class constructor
third inner class constructor
outer class constructor
child constructor
```

The preceding program is with multiple inner class for the parent class and the normal child class.

Program

```
class outer:
def __init__(self):
self.inn1=self.inner1()
self.inn2=self.inner2()
self.inn3=self.inner3()
print("outer class constructor")
class inner1:
def __init__(self):
print("first inner class constructor")
```

```
class inner2:
def __init__(self):
print("second inner class constructor")
class inner3:
def __init__(self):
print("third inner class constructor")

class multi(outer):
def __init__(self):
super().__init__()
self.cinn1=self.multiinner1()
self.cinn2=self.multiinner2()
self.cinn3=self.multiinner3()
print("child constructor")
class multiinner1:
def __init__(self):
print("first child inner class constructor")
class multiinner2:
def __init__(self):
print("second child inner class constructor")
class multiinner3:
def __init__(self):
print("third child inner class constructor")
o=multi()
i1=o.cinn1
i2=o.cinn2
i3=o.cinn3
```

Output

```
first inner class constructor
second inner class constructor
third inner class constructor
outer class constructor
first child inner class constructor
second child inner class constructor
third child inner class constructor
child constructor
```

The preceding program is with multiple inner class for both the parent class and the child class.

Program

```
class outer:
def __init__(self):
self.inn1=self.inner1()
print("outer class constructor")
class inner1:
def __init__(self):
print("inner class constructor")

class multi(outer):
def __init__(self):
super().__init__()
self.cinn1=self.multiinner1()
print("child constructor")
class multiinner1(outer.inner1):
def __init__(self):
super().__init__()
print("child inner class constructor")

o=multi()
i1=o.cinn1
```

Output

```
inner class constructor
outer class constructor
inner class constructor
child inner class constructor
child constructor
```

In the preceding program child inner class inherits parent class inner class.

Solved examples

Program

```
class test:
@staticmethod
def display(i,f,s):
print(i)
print(f)
```

```
print(s)
class sample(test):
pass
sample.display(10,10.123,"python")
```

Output

```
10
10.123
python
```

EXERCISE

1. Print the instance name of the child class.

2. Construct the child class named circle and find the area and the perimeter of the circle with the radius attribute in the parent class.

3. Construct the child class named rectangle and compute the area of the rectangle by taking the length and width attributes in the parent class.

4. Construct the class named multilevel child string and print the string in the uppercase.

5. Construct the class student, class marks, class grade, and print the grade of the student.

6. Create the inner class named age in the outer child class named student, and find the age of the student as per today's date.

## CHAPTER 3

Arrays

The array in python can be created by importing the array module. Arrays are mutable. The elements can be changed or added to the array.

Syntax

*from array import ***

3.1 BYTE ARRAY

Program

```
a = [2, 3, 5, 7]
b = bytearray(a)
print(b)
```

Output

```
bytearray(b'\x02\x03\x05\x07')
```

The preceding program created the byte array b, and the output of the program is the byte array representation.

Program

```
s = "Python is interesting."
a = bytearray(s, 'utf-8')
print(a)
```

DOI: 10.1201/9781003462392-3

```
b = bytearray(s, 'utf-16')
print(b)
```

Output

```
bytearray(b'Python is interesting.')
```

The output of the preceding program is represented in both the utf-8 and utf-16.

Program

```
n = 5
a = bytearray(n)
print(a)
```

Output

```
bytearray(b'\x00\x00\x00\x00\x00')
bytearray(b'\xff\xfeP\x00y\x00t\x00h\x00o\x00n\x00
  \x00i\x00s\x00
\x00i\x00n\x00t\x00e\x00r\x00e\x00s\x00t\x00i\x00n\
  x00g\x00.\x00')
```

The preceding program takes the n value as 5 so the byte array creates 5 values inutf-8 and utf-16.

Program

```
a = bytearray()
print(a)
```

Output

```
bytearray(b")
```

The preceding program created the empty byte array.

Program

```
a = bytearray(b"test")
for i in a:
print(i)
```

```
b = bytearray(b"python testing")
print("Count of t characters is:", b.count(b"t"))
```

Output

```
116
101
115
116
Count of t characters is: 3
```

In the preceding program the for loop prints the byte form of the string test, and the print statement prints the number of occurrences of the character 't' in the string "python testing".

3.2 NUMPY

NumPy is for creating homogeneous n – dimensional arrays.

The syntax for creating 1D array is as follows:

np.array([list of elements])

The syntax for creating 2D array is as follows:

np.array([list of elements][list of elements])

The main advantage of NumPy array is it takes less amount of memory when compared to Python lists.

Program

```
import numpy as np
a=[[1,2],[3,4]]
arr=np.array(a)
print(arr)
```

Output

```
[[1 2]
 [3 4]]
```

The preceding program initializes the array at the time of creating the array and then prints the array elements.

Program

```
import numpy as np
a=np.ones((3,4),dtype=np.int16)
print(a)
```

Output

```
[[1 1 1 1]
[1 1 1 1]
[1 1 1 1]]
```

The preceding program initializes array elements to 1.

Program

```
import numpy as np
a=np.zeros((3,4),dtype=np.int16)
print(a)
```

Output

```
[[0 0 0 0]
 [0 0 0 0]
 [0 0 0 0]]
```

The preceding program initializes array elements to 0.

Program

```
import numpy as np
a=np.ones((3,4),dtype=np.float32)
print(a)
```

Output

```
[[1. 1. 1. 1.]
 [1. 1. 1. 1.]
 [1. 1. 1. 1.]]
```

The preceding program initializes array elements to float 1.0.

Program: Initializing array elements to random numbers

```
import numpy as np
```

```
a=np.random.random((2,2))
print(a)
```

Output

```
[[0.80527886 0.4539138]
 [0.93771029 0.83952726]]
```

The preceding program initializes array elements to random numbers.

Program

```
import numpy as np
a=np.full((3,3),10)
print(a)
```

Output

```
[[10 10 10]
 [10 10 10]
 [10 10 10]]
```

The preceding program initializes array elements to some specific element.

Program

```
import numpy as np
r=int(input("enter array row size"))
c=int(input("enter array column size"))
p=int(input("enter element"))
a=np.full((r,c),p)
print(a)
```

Output

```
enter array row size2
enter array column size3
enter element1
[[111]
 [111]]
```

The preceding program initializes array elements to some specific element taken at run time.

Program

```
import numpy as np
a=np.arange(3,30,5)
print(a)
```

Output

```
[3 8 13 18 23 28]
```

The preceding program arranges the array elements in 1D specific form.

Program

```
import numpy as np
a=np.linspace(3,30,5)
print(a)
```

Output

```
[3.    9.75 16.5   23.25 30.]
```

Program

```
import numpy as np
a=np.eye(3,3)
print(a)
```

Output

```
[[1. 0. 0.]
 [0. 1. 0.]
 [0. 0. 1.]]
```

The preceding program prints the identity matrix in 3 × 3 form.

Program

```
import numpy as np
a=np.eye(3,5)
print(a)
```

Output

```
[[1. 0. 0. 0. 0.]
```

```
[0.  1.  0.  0.  0.]
[0.  0.  1.  0.  0.]]
```

The preceding program prints the identity matrix in 3 × 5 form.

Program: Identity matrix

```
import numpy as np
a=np.identity((3),dtype=np.int16)
print(a)
```

Output

```
[[1 0 0]
 [0 1 0]
 [0 0 1]]
```

The preceding program prints the identity matrix in 3 × 3 form in the specific form, that is, in specific data type (in integer form).

Program: Identity matrix

```
import numpy as np
a=np.identity((5),dtype=np.float32)
print(a)
```

Output

```
[[1.  0.  0.  0.  0.]
 [0.  1.  0.  0.  0.]
 [0.  0.  1.  0.  0.]
 [0.  0.  0.  1.  0.]
 [0.  0.  0.  0.  1.]]
```

The preceding program prints the identity matrix in 5 × 5 form in the specific form, that is, in specific data type (in float form).

Program

```
import numpy as np
a=[[1,2],[3,4]]
arr=np.array(a)
print(arr.size)
```

Output

```
4
```

The preceding program prints the total number of elements in the 2D array.

Program

```
import numpy as np
a=[[1,2,3],[4,5,6]]
arr=np.array(a)
print(arr.size)
```

Output

```
6
```

The preceding program prints the total number of elements in the 2D array.

Program

```
import numpy as np
a=[[1,2,3],[4,5,6]]
arr=np.array(a)
print(arr.ndim)
```

Output

```
2
```

The preceding program prints the total number of dimensions of the 2D array.

Program: 3D array

```
import numpy as np
a=np.zeros((2,2,3),dtype=np.int16)
print(a)
```

Output

```
[[[000]
  [000]]
```

```
[[000]
 [000]]]
```

The preceding program fills the 3D array with the zero value.

Program

```
import numpy as np
a=[[[0, 0, 0],
   [0, 0, 0]],

[[0, 0, 0],
 [0, 0, 0]]]
arr=np.array(a)
print(arr.ndim)
```

Output

```
3
```

The preceding program prints the total number of dimensions of the initialized array.

Program

```
import numpy as np
a=np.zeros((2,2,3),dtype=np.int16)
print(a)
print("Bytes size",a.nbytes)
```

Output

```
[[[0 0 0]
  [0 0 0]]

[[0 0 0]
 [0 0 0]]]
Bytes size 24
```

The preceding program prints the byte size of the array, which was filled with the value zeros.

Program: Length of the array

```
import numpy as np
```

```
a=np.zeros((2,2,3),dtype=np.int16)
print(a)
print("length",len(a))
```

Output

```
[[[0 0 0]
  [0 0 0]]

 [[0 0 0]
  [0 0 0]]]
length 2
```

The preceding program prints the dimensions of the array, which was filled with the value zeros.

Program

```
import numpy as np
a=np.ones((2,2,3),dtype=np.int16)
print(a)
a.astype(float)
print(a)
```

Output

```
[[[1 1 1]
  [1 1 1]]

 [[1 1 1]
  [1 1 1]]]
[[[1 1 1]
  [1 1 1]]

 [[1 1 1]
  [1 1 1]]]
```

3.3 RESHAPING ARRAYS

Reshape changes the shape of the array. By reshaping, the programmers can add dimensions, eliminate dimensions, or can alter the number of the elements in every dimension. The shape of an array is the number of the elements in every dimension.

Program: Reshaping an array into 2D

```
import numpy as np
a=np.arange(24).reshape(3,8)
print(a)
```

Output

```
[[0  1  2  3  4  5  6  7]
 [8  9 10 11 12 13 14 15]
 [16 17 18 19 20 21 22 23]]
```

The preceding program arranged the 24 elements as the 3 × 8 form, that is, three rows and eight columns.

Program

```
import numpy as np
a=np.arange(24).reshape(3,2,4)
print(a)
```

Output

```
[[[0  1  2  3]
  [4  5  6  7]]

[[8  9 10 11]
 [12 13 14 15]]

[[16 17 18 19]
 [20 21 22 23]]]
```

The preceding program reshaping of total 24 elements as an array of 3D.

Program

```
import numpy as np
a=np.array([1,2,3,4,5,6,7,8,9,10,11,12,13,14,15,16])
a.reshape(2,4,2)
```

Output

```
array ([[[ 1,  2],
  [ 3,  4],
```

```
  [ 5,  6],
  [ 7,  8]],
          [[9, 10],
          [11, 12],
          [13, 14],
          [15, 16]]])
```

The preceding program reshapes total 16 elements into 2 × 4 array.

Program: Reshape the array

```
import numpy as np
a=np.array([1,2,3,4,5,6,7,8,9,10,11,12])
a.reshape(3,2,2)
```

Output

```
array ([[[1, 2],
          [3, 4]],

         [[5, 6],
          [7, 8]],

         [[9, 10],
          [11, 12]]])
```

The preceding program reshapes total 12 elements into 3 × 2 array.

Program

```
import numpy as np
a=np.arange(40).reshape(4,2,5)
print(a)
```

Output

```
[[[0 1 2 3 4]
  [5 6 7 8 9]]

 [[10 11 12 13 14]
  [15 16 17 18 19]]

 [[20 21 22 23 24]
  [25 26 27 28 29]]
```

```
[[30 31 32 33 34]
 [35 36 37 38 39]]]
```

The preceding program is about to reshape the array.

Program

```
import numpy as np
a=np.arange(24)
np.hsplit(a,3)
```

Output

```
[array([0, 1, 2, 3, 4, 5, 6, 7]),
array ([8, 9, 10, 11, 12, 13, 14, 15]),
array([16, 17, 18, 19, 20, 21, 22, 23])]
```

Horizontal splitting the array into three equally shaped arrays.

Program

```
import numpy as np
a=np.arange(24)
np.hsplit(a,(3,4))
```

Output

```
[array([0, 1, 2]),
array([3]),
array ([4, 5, 6, 7, 8, 9, 10, 11, 12, 13, 14, 15, 16,
 17, 18, 19, 20, 21, 22, 23])]
```

Split the array after the third and the fourth column of the array.

3.4 OPERATIONS ON ARRAY

We can use different operators on the array.

Program

```
import numpy as np
a=np.array(1,2])
b=np.array([5,6])
a+b
```

Output

```
array([6, 8])
```

The preceding program performed binary addition operator on 1D arrays.

Program

```
import numpy as np
a=np.array([[1,2],[3,4]])
b=np.array([[5,6],[7,8]])
print(a+b)
```

Output

```
[[ 6  8]
 [10 12]]
```

In the preceding program performed binary addition operator on 2D arrays.

Program

```
import numpy as np
a=[[1,2],[3,4]]
b=[[5,6],[7,8]]
np.vstack((a,b))
```

Output

```
array([[1, 2],
[3, 4],
[5, 6],
[7, 8]])
```

The preceding program stacks the array vertically.

Program

```
import numpy as np
a=[[1,2],[3,4]]
b=[[5,6],[7,8]]
np.hstack((a,b))
```

Output

```
array([[l, 2, 5, 6],
[3, 4, 7, 8]])
```

The preceding program stacks the array horizontally.

Program

```
import numpy as np
a=np.array([[1,2],[3,4]])
b=np.array([[5,6],[7,8]])
print(a*b)
```

Output

```
[[5 12]
 [21 32]]
```

The preceding program performed binary multiplication operator on 2D arrays.

Program

```
import numpy as np
a=np.array([[1,2],[3,4]])
print(a*5)
```

Output

```
[[5 10]
[15 20]]
```

The preceding program performed binary addition operator on 2D array with an integer literal.

Program

```
import numpy as np
a=np.array([[1,2],[3,4]])
print("min",a.min())
print("max",a.max())
print("sum",a.sum())
```

Output

```
min 1
max 4
sum 10
```

The preceding program applied the aggregate operators on the 2D array.

Program

```
import numpy as np
a=np.array([[1,2,3],[4,5,6],[7,8,9]])
a.transpose()
```

Output

```
array([[1, 4, 7],
       [2, 5, 8],
       [3, 6, 9]])
```

The preceding program performs the transpose of the matrix.

Program

```
import numpy as np
a=np.array([1,2,3,4,5])
b=np.flip(a)
print(b)
```

Output

```
[5 4 3 2 1]
```

The preceding program performs the reverse the array.

Program

```
import numpy as np
a=np.array([[1,2],[3,4]])
b=np.flip(a)
print(b)
```

Output

```
[[4 3]
 [2 1]]
```

The preceding program performs the reverse the array.

Program

```
import numpy as np
a=np.array([[1,2,3],[4,5,6],[7,8,9]])
b=np.flip(a)
print(b)
```

Output

```
[[9 8 7]
 [6 5 4]
 [3 2 1]]
```

The preceding program performs the reverse the array.

Program

```
import numpy as np
a=np.array([[1,2,3,4],[6,7,8,9],[10,11,12,13]])
b=np.flip(a)
print(b)
```

Output

```
[[13 12 11 10]
 [9 8 7 6]
 [4 3 2 1]]
```

The preceding program performs the reverse the array.

Program

```
import numpy as np
a=np.array([[1,2,3,4],[6,7,8,9],[10,11,12,13]])
b=a.copy()
b[1]=np.flip(a[1])
print(b)
```

Output

```
[[1 2 3 4]
 [9 8 7 6]
 [10 11 12 13]]
```

The preceding program performs the reverse the array.

Program

```
import numpy as np
a=np.array([[1,2,3,4],[6,7,8,9],[10,11,12,13]])
b=np.flip(a,axis=1)
print(b)
```

Output

```
[[4 3 2 1]
 [9 8 7 6]
 [13 12 11 10]]
```

The preceding program performs the reverse the array.

Program

```
import numpy as np
a=np.array([[1,2,3,4],[6,7,8,9],[10,11,12,13]])
b=np.flip(a,axis=0)
print(b)
```

Output

```
[[10 11 12 13]
 [ 6  7  8  9]
 [ 1  2  3  4]]
```

The preceding program performs the reverse the array.

Program

```
import numpy as np
a=np.array([[1,2,3,4],[6,7,8,9],[10,11,12,13]])
b[1:,]=np.flip(a[1:,])
print(b)
```

Output

```
[[10 11 12 13]
 [13 12 11 10]
 [ 9  8  7  6]]
```

The preceding program performs the reverse the column at index position 1.

Program

```
import numpy as np
a=np.array([[1,2,3,4],[6,7,8,9],[10,11,12,13]])
a.flatten()
```

Output

```
array ([1,    2,     3,    4,    6,    7,    8,    9,
10,   11,   12,    13])
```

The preceding program performs the flatten the array to 1D.

Program

```
import numpy as np
a=np.array([[1,2,3,4],[6,7,8,9],[10,11,12,13]])
b=a.copy()
print(b)
b[1][1]=99
print(b)
print(a)
```

Output

```
[[ 1   2   3   4]
 [ 6   7   8   9]
 [10  11  12  13]]
[[ 1   2   3   4]
 [ 6  99   8   9]
 [10  11  12  13]]
[[ 1   2   3   4]
 [ 6   7   8   9]
[10  11  12  13]]
```

The preceding program performing the modification to the copied will not reflect on the original array.

Program

```
import numpy as np
```

```
a=np.array([1,2,3,4,5])
print(a)
b=a.ravel()
b[4]=99
print(b)
print(a)
```

Output

```
[1 2 3 4 5]
[1 2 3 4 99]
[1 2 3 4 99]
```

The preceding program performing the modifications in the copied array reflects on the original array.

Program

```
import numpy as np
a=np.array([[1,2,3]])
print(a)
np.swapaxes(a,0,1)
```

Output

```
[[123]]
array([[1],
    [2],
        [3]])
```

The preceding program performs the swap spaces of the array.

Program

```
import numpy as np
a=np.arange(12).reshape(3,4)
print(a)
np.swapaxes(a,1,0)
```

Output

```
[[0   1    2    3]
 [4 5  6   7]
  [8 9 10 11]]
```

```
array ([[0, 4, 8],
  [1, 5, 9],
  [2, 6, 10],
  [3, 7, 11]])
```

The preceding program performs the swap spaces of the array.

Program

```
import numpy as np
a=np.array([[[0,1,2],[3,4,5],[6,7,8],[9,10,11]]])
print(a)
np.swapaxes(a,0,2)
```

Output

```
[[[0 1 2]
[3 4 5]]
[[6 7 8]
[9 10 11]]]

array ([[[0, 6],
[3, 9]],
[[1, 7],
[4, 10]],

[[2, 8],
[5, 11]]])
```

The preceding program performs the swap axes.

Program

```
import numpy as np
a=np.array([[[0,1,2],[3,4,5]],[[6,7,8],[9,10,11]]])
print(a)
np.swapaxes(a,0,1)
```

Output

```
[[[ 0  1  2]
  [ 3  4  5]]

 [[ 6  7  8]
  [ 9 10 11]]]
```

```
array ([[[0, 1, 2],
    [6, 7, 8]],

[[3, 4, 5],
[9, 10, 11]]])
```

The preceding program performs the swap axes.

Program

```
import numpy as np
a=np.array([[[0,1,2],[3,4,5]],[[6,7,8],[9,10,11]]])
print(a)
np.swapaxes(a,1,2)
```

Output

```
[[[0 1 2]
[3 4 5]]

[[6 7 8]
[9 10 11]]]
array ([[[0, 3],
        [1, 4],

        [2, 5]],

[[6, 9],
[7, 10],
[8, 11]]])
```

The preceding program performs the swap axes.

Program

```
import numpy as np
a=np.array([[[0,1,2],[3,4,5]],[[6,7,8],[9,10,11]]])
print(a)
np.swapaxes(a,2,1)
```

Output

```
[[[ 0 1 2]
  [ 3 4 5]]
```

```
[[ 6  7  8]
 [ 9 10 11]]]

array ([[[0, 3],
         [1, 4],
         [2, 5]],

[[6,  9],
[7, 10],
[8, 11]]])
```

The preceding program performs the swap axes.

Program

```
import numpy as np
a=np.array([[1,2],[6,7,8,9],[10]])
print(a)
```

Output

```
[list([1, 2]) list([6, 7, 8, 9]) list([10])]
```

The preceding program performs the jagged arrays.

Program

```
from numpy import *
n=int(input("enter array size"))
a=zeros(n,dtype=int)
for i in range(n):
      p=int(input("Number:"))
      a[i]=p
print(a)
```

Output

```
enter array size2
Number:1
Number:2
[1 2]
```

The preceding program takes the user input in the NumPy array.

Program

```
from numpy import *
r=int(input("enter array row size"))
c=int(input("enter array col size"))
a=[]
for i in range(r):
  m=[]
  for j in range(c):
  m.append(int(input("Number:")))
a.append(m)
      for i in range(r):
              for j in range(c):
              print(a[i][j],end=" ")
        print()
```

Output

```
enter array row size3
enter array col size2
Number:1
Number:2
Number:3
Number:4
Number:5
Number:6
1 2
3 4
5 6
```

The preceding program takes the user input in the NumPy 2D array.

Program

```
import numpy as np
r=int(input("enter array row size"))
c=int(input("enter array col size"))
print("enter",r*c," first array elements")
a=list(map(int,input().split()))
arr=np.array(a).reshape(r,c)
print(arr)
print("enter",r*c," second array elements")
b=list(map(int,input().split()))
```

```
brr=np.array(b).reshape(r,c)
print(brr)
arr+brr
```

Output

```
enter array row size2
enter array col size3
enter 6 first array elements
1 2 3 4 5 6
[[1 2 3]
 [4 5 6]]
enter 6 second array elements
7 8 9 10 11 12
[[7 8 9]
 [10 11 12]]
array ([[8, 10, 12],
[14, 16, 18]])
```

The preceding program performs the NumPy array addition.

Program

```
import numpy as np
r=int(input("enter array row size"))
c=int(input("enter array col size"))
print("enter",r*c," first array elements")
a=list(map(int,input().split()))
arr=np.array(a).reshape(r,c)
print(arr)
print("enter",r*c," second array elements")
  b=list(map(int,input().split()))
brr=np.array(b).reshape(r,c)
print(brr)
print("matrix subtraction result")
arr-brr
```

Output

```
enter array row size2
enter array col size2
enter 4 first array elements
1 2 3 4
[[1 2]
```

```
 [3 4]]
enter 4 second array elements
5 6 7 8
[[5 6]
 [7 8]]
matrix subtraction result
array([[-4, -4],
       [-4, -4]])
```

The preceding program performs the matrix subtraction.

Program

```
import numpy as np
r=int(input("enter array row size"))
c=int(input("enter array col size"))
print("enter",r*c," first array elements")
a=list(map(int,input().split()))
arr=np.array(a).reshape(r,c)
print(arr)
print("enter",r*c," second array elements")
  b=list(map(int,input().split())) brr=np.array(b).
  reshape(r,c)
print(brr)
print("matrix multiplication result")
arr*brr
```

Output

```
enter array row size2
enter array col size2
enter 4 first array elements
1 2 3 4
[[1 2]
 [3 4]]
enter 4 second array elements
5 6 7 8
[[5 6]
 [7 8]]
matrix multiplication result
array ([[ 5, 12],
        [21, 32]])
```

The preceding program performs the matrix multiplication.

Program

```
import numpy as np
a=np.array([1,2,3,4,5])
b=np.array([1,2,7,8,9])
a==b
```

Output

```
array ([True, True, False, False, False])
```

The preceding program performs the array equality.

Program

```
import numpy as np
a=np.array([1,2,3,4,5])
b=np.array([1,2,7,8,9])
np.array_equal(a,b)
```

Output

```
False
```

The preceding program performs the array equality.

Program

```
import numpy as np
a=np.array([1,2,3,4,5])
b=np.array([1,2,3,4,5])
np.array_equal(a,b)
```

Output

```
True
```

The preceding program performs the array equality.

Program

```
import numpy as np
a=np.array([1,1,0,0,0],dtype=bool)
```

```
b=np.array([1,1,0,0,1],dtype=bool)
print(np.logical_or(a,b))
print(np.logical_and(a,b))
```

Output

```
[True True False False True]
[True True False False False]
```

The preceding program performs the logical operations on NumPy array.

Program

```
import numpy as np
a=np.arange(5)
print(np.sin(a))
print(np.cos(a))
print(np.tan(a))
print(np.exp(a))
print(np.log(a))
```

Output

```
[0.     0.84147098 0.90929743 0.14112001 -0.7568025]
[1.     0.54030231 -0.41614684 -0.9899925 -0.65364362]
[0.     1.55740772 -2.18503986 -0.14254654 1.15782128]
[1.     2.71828183 7.3890561 20.08553692 54.59815003]
[      -inf 0.     0.69314718 1.09861229 1.38629436]
```

The preceding program performs the trigonometric functions on NumPy array.

Program

```
import numpy as np
a=np.array([[1,2,3,4],[6,7,8,9],[10,11,12,13]])
print(a)
print("vertical sum")
print(np.sum(a,axis=0))
print(" horizontal sum")
print(np.sum(a,axis=1))
```

Output

```
[[ 1   2   3   4]
 [ 6   7   8   9]
 [10 11 12 13]]
vertical sum
 [17 20 23 26]
horizontal sum
 [10 30 46]
```

The preceding program performs the sum on 2D array.

Program

```
import numpy as np
a=np.array([1,2,3,4,5,6,7,8,9,10,11,12])
print("mean:",a.mean())
print("median",np.median(a))
```

Output

```
mean: 6.5
median 6.5
```

The preceding program performs the mean and median of array.

Program

```
import numpy as np
a=np.array([[1,2,3,4],[6,7,8,9],[10,11,12,13]])
print("mean:",a.mean())
print("median",np.median(a))
```

Output

```
mean: 7.166666666666667
median 7.5
```

The preceding program performs the mean and median of 2D array.

Program

```
import numpy as np
a=np.array([[1,2],[6,7]],dtype=complex)
print(a)
```

Output

```
[[1.+0.j 2.+0.j]
 [6.+0.j 7.+0.j]]
```

The preceding program represents the array as the complex type.

Program

```
import numpy as np
a=np.array([1,2,3,4,5,6,7,8,9,10,11,12])
print("correlation coefficient:",np corrcoef(a))
print("standard deviation",np.std(a))
```

Output

```
correlation coefficient: 1.0
standard deviation 3.452052529534663
```

The preceding program performs the aggregate functions.

Program

```
import numpy as np
a=np.array([[1,2,3,4],[6,7,8,9],[10,11,12,13]])
print("correlation coefficient:",np corrcoef(a))
print("standard deviation",np.std(a))
```

Output

```
correlation coefficient: [[1. 1. 1.]
[1. 1. 1.]
[1. 1. 1.]]
standard deviation 3.8477987935383986
```

The preceding program performs the aggregate functions.

EXERCISE

1. Count the number of occurrences of the specified element in the array.

2. Insert the array element at the specified index.

3. Convert the array to the list.

4. Create a Boolean array.

5. Print the odd index elements of the array.

6. Replace the array element at the specified position with the new value.

7. Stack three array horizontally.

8. Extract the elements of the array within the specified range.

9. Compare two arrays.

10. Reverse the columns of the array.

## CHAPTER 4

Exception Handling

An exception is an unusual situation that terminates the execution of the program. Whenever an exception happens, the program blocks the execution. There is a way to handle the exception. An exception is the runtime error that is incompetent to handle to Python program. If there is no code to deal with the exception, the interpreter doesn't execute the code that appears after the exception.

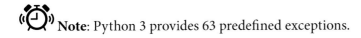 **Note**: Python 3 provides 63 predefined exceptions.

If an exception arises inside the try block, the control jumps to the first instruction of the except block. There must be at least a single except for every try statement, and the except statement should not be used without a preceding try statement. After executing the except block, the control never jumps back to the try block, and if one except block is executed, then the remaining except block of the specified try statements will not be executed. If none of the specified except branches matches the raised exception, the execution remains unhandled. The unnamed except block should be the last block for the try statement. If there is no matching except block for the raised exception, then the compiler takes care and terminates the program. At the time of catching the exception, the general exception should be placed before the concrete exceptions.

DOI: 10.1201/9781003462392-4

4.1 EXCEPTION HANDLING IN PYTHON

The try except statement:

Python offers try blocks to facilitate exception handling. A try block comprises of keyword try, which includes statements that could cause exceptions and statements that should be omitted if an exception occurs. Exceptions may surface beyond unambiguously mentioned code in a try block, through calls to other functions and through deeply nested function calls originated by code in a try block. Exceptions are processed by an exception handler block, which catch and handle exceptions. At least one except block should immediately go after each try block. Each catch handler starts with the keyword except followed by exception parameter that represents the type of exception the exception handler can handle. When an exception arises in a try block, the exception handler that implements is the one whose type fits the type of exception that happened. If an exception parameter comprises of an optional parameter name, the catch handler can utilize that parameter name to cooperate with a caught exception object in the body of the exception handler.

The try block must be followed with the except statement, which comprises a block of code that will be executed if there is an exception in the try block. The except blocks are searched in the same order in which they appear in the code, and the programmer must not use more than one except branch with a specified exception name.

⏰ **Note:** Placing between a statement between try block and its corresponding exception handler is a syntax error.

⏰ **Note**: Each exception handler can have only a single parameter.

⏰ **Note**: Catching the same type of error in two distinct exception handlers following a single try block is a logical error.

⏰ **Note**: Control never returns to the first statement following the throw point. With exception handling, a program can continue executing after dealing the exception.

🕐 **Note:** Throwing an exception that has not been stated in the exception handlers triggers a call to the unexcepted functions.

Syntax-1

```
try
[suspicious erroneous code]
except:
[run this code if an exception occurs]
```

Syntax-2

```
try
[suspicious erroneous code]
except Exception:
[run this code if an exception occurs]
```

Program

```
try:
a=int(input("enter integer"))
b=int(input("enter integer"))
print(a/b)
except:
print("exception occurred")
```

Output

```
enter integer10
enter integer0
exception occurred
```

The preceding program using try except statement with no specified exception.

The except keyword starts a piece of code that will be executed if the code inside the try block goes wrong.

Program

```
try:
a=int(input("enter integer"))
b=int(input("enter integer"))
```

```
print(a/b)
except Exception as e:
print(e)
```

Output

```
enter integer5
enter integer0
division by zero
```

The preceding program uses try except statement with specified exception.

4.2 SINGLE TRY MULTIPLE EXCEPT STATEMENTS

There may be the possibility that more than one exception can occur in a single program. This issue can be solved by writing more than one consecutive try-except blocks, one for each possible exception.

Syntax

```
try
[suspicious erroneous code]
except excedption1:
[run this code if an exception occurs]
except excedption2:
[run this code if an exception occurs]
```

Program

```
try:
i=int(input("enter integer"))
j=int(input("enter integer"))
print(i/j)
except ZeroDivisionError as e:
print(e.__class__)
except ValueError as e:
print(e.__class__)
except:
print("error")
enter integer5
enter integer0
<class 'ZeroDivisionError'>
```

The preceding program uses the single try and multiple exception.

Program

```
try:
i=int(input("enter integer"))
j=int(input("enter integer"))
print(i/j)
except:
pass
```

Output

```
enter integer5
enter integer0
```

The preceding program uses writing pass in the exception handler.

No error message is not printed in the preceding program, just used the pass no statement. Handled the exception but no message has not been printed because there is no message statement in the except block.

Program

```
a= [0,0.0,'1']
for i in a:
try:
print("element:", i)
print(1/i)
except Exception as e:
print(e.__class__)
```

Output

```
element: 0
<class 'ZeroDivisionError'>
element: 0.0
<class 'ZeroDivisionError'>
element: 1
<class 'TypeError'>
```

The preceding program uses the single try multiple exceptions in single except statement.

Program

```
try:
print("try block")
print("between try and except")
except:
print("except block")
```

Output

```
File "<ipython-input-21-3e44f9eab93f>", line 3
print("between try and except")
      ^

SyntaxError: invalid syntax
```

The preceding program uses the statement between the try and the except statement. It throws the error because placed a statement between the try and except.

Program

```
try:
i=int(input("enter integer"))
j=int(input("enter integer"))
print(i/j)
except (ValueError,ZeroDivisionError)as e:
print(e.__class__)
```

Output 1

```
enter integer5
enter integer0
<class 'ZeroDivisionError'>
```

The preceding program uses the single try single except but handling multiple exceptions with single except.

4.3 SINGLE TRY SINGLE EXCEPT WITH MULTIPLE EXCEPTIONS STATEMENTS

Python permits to declare the multiple exceptions with the except statement. Declaring multiple exceptions is effective in the class when a try block throws multiple exceptions.

```
try
[suspicious erroneous code]
except (exception1, exception2 . . . exception N):
[run this code if an any of the exception occurs]
```

If an exception is raised inside the function, the exception can be handled either inside or outside the function.

Program

```
a,b=1,0
try:
print(a/b)
print("This won't be printed")
print('10'+10)
except TypeError:
print("you added values of incompatible types")
except ZeroDivisionError:
print("You divided by 0")
```

Output

```
You divided by 0
```

The preceding program uses the single try single except with multiple exceptions statements.

Program

```
def test():
try:
print('try')
except:
print('caught exception')
else:
print('no exception raised')
finally:
print('finally')
test()
```

Output

```
try
```

```
no exception raised
finally
```

The preceding program uses the try except else finally program.

Program

```
def test():
try:
1/0
except:
print('caught exception')
else:
print('no exception raised')
finally:
print('finally')
test()
```

Output

```
caught exception
finally
```

The preceding program handles the exception inside the function.

4.4 TRY-EXCEPT-ELSE

In Python, there is the possibility of using the else statement with the try-except statement, in which the else block will be executed if no exception appears in the try block.

Syntax

```
try:
[suspicious erroneous code]
except:
[run this code if an exception occurs]
else:
[run this code if no except block is executed]
```

Program

```
def test(x, y):
try:
```

```
r = x // y
except ZeroDivisionError:
print("ZeroDivisionError ")
else:
print("Result:", r)
test(10,3)
test(5,0)
```

Output

```
Result: 3
ZeroDivisionError
```

The preceding program uses the try-except-else.

4.5 THE TRY . . . FINALLY BLOCK

Python supports the optional finally statement, which is applied with the try statement.

Syntax

```
try:
[suspicious erroneous code]
finally:
[finally block always execute]
```

Program: try else finally

```
try:
print("inside try")
except:
print("error handled")
else:
print("else try block")
finally:
print("finally block")
```

Output

```
inside try
else try block
finally block
```

The preceding program uses the try-except-else-finally.

Program: try else finally block

```
try:
i=int(input("enter integer"))
if i<0:
raise ValueError("value is negative")
else:
print("value:",i)
except ValueError as e:
print(e)
```

Output

```
enter integer-1
value is negative
```

The preceding program uses the try-except-else.

4.6 RAISING EXCEPTIONS

An exception can be raised by using the raise keyword in python. To elevate the exception, the raise statement is used. The exception class name follows it and an exception that can be presented with a value in the parentheses.

Syntax

```
raise exception[value]
```

Program: Raise the exception with the no message
```
try:
raise
except:
print("error occurred")
```

Output

```
error occurred
```

Program

```
i = int(input("Enter a positive number: "))

if i<0:
raise Exception("Please enter only positive value ")

print("value = ", i)
```

Output

```
Enter a positive number: -5
--------------------------------------------------------------
Exception                            Traceback (most
  recent call last)
<ipython-input-8-27485c90c2d3> in <module>()
      2
      3 if i<0:
----> 4 raise Exception("Please enter only positive
  value ")
      5
      6 print("value = ", i)
Exception: Please enter only positive value
```

The preceding program raises the exception with the message.

Note: Simply raise the raise without message can be used inside the function only, otherwise raises (sentence recheck).

An exception

Program: Try except else clause

```
try:
i=int(input("enter integer"))
if i<0:
raise ValueError("value is negative")
else:
print("value:",i)
except ValueError as e:
print(e)
else:
print("else block")
```

Output

```
enter integer-5
value is negative
```

Program

```
def test():
try:
```

```
raise
except:
print("error handled inside function")
raise
try:
test()
except:
print("error handled in main")
```

Output

```
error handled inside function
error handled in main
```

Program

```
def test():
i=int(input("enter integer"))
j=int(input("enter integeer"))
print(i/j)
try:
test()
except Exception as e:
print("error handled in main",e.__class__)
```

Output

```
enter integer5
enter integeer0
error handled in main <class 'ZeroDivisionError'>
```

The preceding program handles the error in main.

4.7 USER-DEFINED EXCEPTIONS

In Python the users have the ability to raise their own exceptions.

Program

```
class test(Exception):
pass
try:
raise test("my exception")
except test as t:
print(t)
```

Output

```
my exception
```

The preceding program uses the user-defined exception.

Program

```
class negative(Exception):
def __init__(self,s):
self.s=s
super().__init__(self.s)
while(True):
n=int(input("enter number"))
try:
if n<=0:
raise negative("should enter positive number")
else:
print("Number:",n)
break
except negative as e:
print(e)
```

Output

```
enter number0
should enter positive number
enter number-5
should enter positive number
enter number5
Number: 5
```

The preceding program invoking parent class constructor in user-defined exceptions.

4.8 CONSTRUCTORS IN EXCEPTION HANDLING

The users can use the exception handling in the class constructors.

Program

```
class test:
def __init__(self,n):
try:
```

```
if n<0:
raise ValueError("value is negative")
else:
self.n=n
except ValueError as e:
print(e)
t=test(100)
print(t.n)
```

Output

```
100
```

The preceding program used the try except in constructor.

Program: Error handling in constructor

```
class test:
def __init__(self,n):
try:
if n<0:
raise ValueError("value is negative")
else:
print("value:",n)
except ValueError as e:
print(e)
t=test(-1)
```

Output

```
value is negative
```

The preceding program used the try except else in constructor.

4.8.1 Exception and Inheritance

Various exception classes in Python can be derived from a common base called the exception class. Using inheritance with exception enables an exception handler to catch related error of the subclass exceptions also. If a catch handler catches a reference to an exception object of a parent class type, it also catches the references of all the objects of classes derived from that parent class.

Syntax

```
class test(exception):
#test class body
```

Program

```
class parent(Exception):
def __init__(self, offer):
self.offerName = offer[0]
self.offerType = offer[1]
self.st = self._construct_message()
super(parent, self).__init__(self.st)

def _construct_message(self):
return 'parent'.format(self.offerName)

class derived(parent):
def _construct_message(self):
return 'derived'.format(self.offerName, self.
  offerType)
```

EXERCISE

1. Write a Python program to catch multiple exceptions in a single except statement.

2. Write a Python program to raise an exception if number is greater than 100.

3. Write a Python program to raise an exception if number is negative number.

## CHAPTER 5

Multi Threading

A thread is a flow of execution. Multi threading helps to run multiple tasks simultaneously.

Advantages of multi threading:

1. Simplifies the code

2. Better utilization of resources

3. Allows and parallel concurrent programming

4. Increases the performance

5. Reduces the response time

Multi threading can be done by three ways in Python:

1. Without class

2. Subclass to thread class

3. Use class concept but not subclass to thread class

5.1 MULTIPROCESSING IN PYTHON

Python provides the multiprocessing module to perform multiple tasks within the single system.

DOI: 10.1201/9781003462392-5

Program

```
from multiprocessing import Process
def f():
print('with out arguments')
p = Process(target=f, args=())
p.start()
p.join()
```

Output

```
with out arguments
```

The preceding program performs the multiprocessing without arguments.

Program: Multiprocessing with arguments

```
from multiprocessing import Pool
def test(x):
return x*x
with Pool(5) as t:
print(t.map(test, [1, 2, 3, 4, 5]))
```

Output

```
[1, 4, 9, 16, 25]
```

The preceding program performs the multiprocessing with arguments.

Program: Number of CPU working

```
import multiprocessing
import os
print(multiprocessing.cpu_count())
print(os. cpu_count())
```

Output

```
2
2
```

The preceding program calculates the number of CPU running at that instant.

5.2 MULTI THREADING

There are two ways to handle threads in Python:

1. The thread module

2. The threading module

5.2.1 Starting a New Thread

Syntax

```
Thread.start_new_thread(function,args[,kwargs])
Parameters:
function-
args-
kwargs-
```

Program: Starting a new thread

The Threading Module

Methods	Description
threading.activecount()	Returns count of threads active threads
threading.currentthread()	Returns current thread information
run()	Activity of the thread
start()	Stars the thread
Join([time])	Until the thread that called join() was terminated, the CPU blocks the remaining threads
isAlive()	Checks if the thread is alive or not
getName()	Returns the name of the running thread
setName()	Sets the name of the thread
threading.enumerate	Returns the list of all active threads

5.3 CREATING THREAD USING THREADING MODULE

To apply a new thread using the threading module using the threading module:

1. Define a new subclass of the thread class.

2. Override the __init__(self[,args]) method to add the arguments.

3. Override the run(self[,args]) method to implement what the thread.

When starting the new thread by invoking the start(), which in turn calls run() method.

Program

```
import threading
def test():
print("test method")

t1 = threading.Thread(target=test)
t1.start()
```

Output

```
test method
```

The preceding program is a very simple program to start a thread.

Program

```
import threading
def test():
print("inside test function")
for i in range(5):
print("test i=",i)
t1=threading.Thread(target=test)
t1.start()
```

Output

```
inside test function
test i= 0
test i= 1
test i= 2
test i= 3
test i= 4
```

The preceding program creates a single thread without passing arguments.

Program

```
import threading
def test():
print("inside test function")
```

```
for i in range(5):
print("test i=",i)
def sample():
print("inside sample fumction")
for i in range(5):
print("sample i=",i)
t1=threading.Thread(target=test)
t2=threading.Thread(target=sample)
t1.start()
t2.start()
```

Output

```
inside test function
inside sample fumctiontest i=
sample i= 0
test i= 1
test i= 2
test i= 3
test i= 4
0
sample i= 1
sample i= 2
sample i= 3
sample i= 4
```

The preceding program creates two threads without passing arguments.

Program

```
import threading
def test(n):
print("inside test fumction")
for i in range(n):
print("test i=",i)
def sample(n):
print("inside sample fumction")
for i in range(n):
print("sample i=",i)
t1=threading.Thread(target=test,args=(5,))
t2=threading.Thread(target=sample,args=(7,))
t1.start()
t2.start()
```

Output

```
inside test fumction
inside sample fumction
sample i=test i= 0
test i= 1
test i= 2
test i= 3
test i= 4
0
sample i= 1
sample i= 2
sample i= 3
sample i= 4
sample i= 5
sample i= 6
```

The preceding program creates two threads with passing arguments.

Program

```
import threading
def test():
print("inside test fumction")
print("thread name:",threading.current_thread().name)
def sample():
print("inside sample fumction")
print("thread name:",threading.current_thread().name)
t1=threading.Thread(target=test,name="test")
t2=threading.Thread(target=sample,name="sample")
t1.start()
t2.start()
```

Output

```
inside test fumction
thread name: test
inside sample fumction
thread name: sample
```

In the preceding program the name of the two threads are set and printing the thread name.

Program

```
import threading
def test():
print("inside test function")
for i in range(5):
print("test i=",i)
def sample():
print("inside sample fumction")
for i in range(5):
print("sample i=",i)
t1=threading.Thread(target=test)
t2=threading.Thread(target=sample)
t1.start()
t2.start()
t1.join()
t2.join()
```

Output

```
inside test function
test i= 0
test i= 1
test i= 2
test i= 3
test i= 4
inside sample fumction
sample i= 0
sample i= 1
sample i= 2
sample i= 3
sample i= 4
```

In the preceding program the join() method is used, which blocks the remaining threads until the current thread completes its task.

Program

```
import threading
import time
def test():
print("inside test function")
```

```
for i in range(5):
print("test i=",i)
time.sleep(2)
t1=threading.Thread(target=test)
t1.start()
```

Output

```
inside test function
test i= 0
```

The preceding program used the sleep method to put the thread ideal for specified time.

Program

```
import threading
import time
def test():
print("inside test fumction")
for i in range(5):
print("test i=",i)
time.sleep(2)
def sample():
print("inside sample fumction")
for i in range(5):
print("sample i=",i)
time.sleep(2)
t1=threading.Thread(target=test)
t2=threading.Thread(target=sample)
t1.start()
t2.start()
```

Output

```
inside test fumction
test i= 0
inside sample fumction
sample i= 0
```

The preceding program used the threads and the sleep method in those two threads to put the thread ideal for specified time.

Program

```
import threading
import time
class test(threading.Thread):
def run(self):
for i in range(7):
print("run() method",i)

for i in range(5):
print("run method",i)
t=test()
t.start()
```

Output

```
run method 0
run method 1
run method 2
run method 3
run method 4
run() method 0
run() method 1
run() method 2
run() method 3
run() method 4
run() method 5
run() method 6
```

The preceding program used the run() method to execute the thread.

Program

```
import threading
from threading import *
import time
def test(n):
for i in range(n):
time.sleep(2)

def sample(n):
for i in range(n):
time.sleep(2)

start=time.time()
n=int(input("enter integer"))
```

```
t1=Thread(target=test,args=(n,))
t2=Thread(target=sample,args=(n,))
t1.start()
t2.start()
end=time.time()
print("time to execute",(end-start))
```

Output

```
enter integer5
time to execute 20.022241592407227
```

The preceding program calculates the time to start a thread and the thread execution.

Program

```
import threading
import time
class test(threading.Thread):
def run(self):
for i in range(5):
print("test run()",i)
class sample(threading.Thread):
def run(self):
for i in range(5):
print(" sample run()",i)

t=test()
s=sample()
t.start()
s.start()
t.join()
s.join()
```

Output

```
test run() 0
test run() 1
test run() 2
test run() 3
test run() 4
sample run() 0
sample run() 1
sample run() 2
```

```
sample run() 3
sample run() 4
```

In the preceding program the join() method is used, which blocks the remaining threads until the current thread completes its task.

5.4 SYNCHRONIZING THE THREAD

In Python, a lock is started by invoking the lock() method, which returns the new lock. The release() method of the new lock object is exploited to release the lock when it is no longer needed.

```
import threading
import os

def test1():
print("test 1 assigned to thread:
  {}".format(threading.current_thread().name))
print("ID of process running test 1:
  {}".format(os.getpid()))

def test2():
print("test 2 assigned to thread: {}".
  format(threading.current_thread().name))
print("ID of process running test 2: {}".format(os.
  getpid()))

if __name__ == "__main__":

# print ID of current process
print("ID of process running main program: {}".
  format(os.getpid()))

# print name of main thread
print("Main thread name:
  {}".format(threading.current_thread().name))

# creating threads
t1 = threading.Thread(target=test1, name='t1')
t2 = threading.Thread(target=test2, name='t2')
# starting threads

t1.start()
t2.start()
```

```
# wait until all threads finish
t1.join()
t2.join()
```

Output

```
ID of process running main program: 63
Main thread name: MainThread
test 1 assigned to thread: t1
ID of process running test 1: 63
test 2 assigned to thread: t2
ID of process running test 2: 63
```

Program

```python
1  import threading
   class test(object):
3      def __init__(self, start = 0):
4          self.lock = threading.Lock()
5          self.value = start
6      def inc(self):
7          self.lock.acquire()
8          try:
9              self.value = self.value + 1
10         finally:
11             self.lock.release()
12 c = test()
13 t = threading.Thread(target=c.inc)
14 t.start()
15 print(c.value)
```

5.4.1 Race Condition

When more than one thread is trying to access the shared variable simultaneously, then the race condition will raise.

Step 1: The shared variable is initialized, and it is accessing in the inc() function

```python
import threading
# global variable x
x = 0

def inc():
"""
function to increment global variable x
```

```
"""
global x
x += 1
```

Step 2: Calling the shared variable function

```
def test1():
"""
task for thread
calls increment function 100000 times.
"""
for _ in range(100000):
inc()
```

Step 3: Reassigning the shared variable

```
def test2():
global x
# setting global variable x as 0
x = 0
```

Step 4: Starting the thread

```
# creating threads
t1 = threading.Thread(target=test1)
t2 = threading.Thread(target=test1)
# start threads
t1.start()
t2.start()
# wait until threads finish their job
t1.join()
t2.join()
```

Step 5: Calling main and accessing the shared variable

```
if __name__ == "__main__":
for i in range(10):
test2()
print("Iteration {0}: x = {1}".format(i,x))
```

Output

```
Iteration 0: x = 168820
Iteration 1: x = 200000
Iteration 2: x = 163939
```

```
Iteration 3: x = 200000
Iteration 4: x = 200000
Iteration 5: x = 200000
Iteration 6: x = 200000
Iteration 7: x = 200000
Iteration 8: x = 200000
Iteration 9: x = 169937
```

5.4.2 Locks

To avoid race conditions, locks were introduced.

The functioning of the locks can be done in three ways:

1. First, acquire lock on the shared variable.

2. Process the shared variable.

3. Release the lock.

Step 1: The shared variable is initialized, and it is accessing in the inc() function

```
import threading
# global variable x
x = 0
def inc():
"""
function to increment global variable x
"""
global x
x += 1
```

Step 2: Before calling the shared variable function, the lock was acquired, and after the processing, the lock has been released

```
def test1(lock):
"""
task for thread
calls increment function 100000 times.
"""
for _ in range(100000):
lock.acquire()
increment()
lock.release()
```

Step 3: Reassigning the shared variable

```
def test2():
global x
# setting global variable x as 0
x = 0
```

Step 4: Starting the thread and the lock

```
# creating a lock
lock = threading.Lock()

# creating threads
t1 = threading.Thread(target=test1, args=(lock,))
t2 = threading.Thread(target=test1, args=(lock,))

# start threads
t1.start()
t2.start()

# wait until threads finish their job
t1.join()
t2.join()
```

Step 5: Calling main and accessing the shared variable

```
if __name__ == "__main__":
for i in range(10):
test2()
print("Iteration {0}: x = {1}".format(i,x))
```

Output

```
Iteration 0: x = 200000
Iteration 1: x = 200000
Iteration 2: x = 200000
Iteration 3: x = 200000
Iteration 4: x = 200000
Iteration 5: x = 200000
Iteration 6: x = 200000
Iteration 7: x = 200000
Iteration 8: x = 200000
Iteration 9: x = 200000
```

Pooling

Thread pool helps to achieve the concurrency of the execution of the threads.

```python
# Python program to understand the concept of pool
import multiprocessing
import os

def square(n):
print("process id for {0}: {1}".format(n,
  os.getpid()))
return (n*n)

if __name__ == "__main__":
# input list
a = [1,2,3,-1,-2]
# creating a pool object
p = multiprocessing.Pool()

# map list to target function
r = p.map(square,a)

print(r)
```

Output

```
process id for 1: 369
process id for 3: 369
process id for -1: 369
process id for -2: 369
process id for 2: 370
[1, 4, 9, 1, 4]
```

5.4.3 Semaphore

Semaphore provides the thread synchronization to use the thread resources. The operations that are using to use and release the semaphore is the acquire() and release(). The acquire() methods decrements the semaphores values, and the release increments the semaphore value.

Program

```python
# importing the modules
from threading import *
import time
```

```
# creating thread instance where count = 3
obj = Semaphores(3)

# creating instance
def test(s):

# calling acquire method
obj.acquire()
for i in range(5):
print('testing \n', end = ' ')
time.sleep(1)
print(s)

# calling release method
obj.release()

# creating multiple thread
t1 = Thread(target = test, args = ('T-1',))
t2 = Thread(target = test, args = ('T-2',))

# calling the threads
t1.start()
t2.start()
```

Output

```
testing
testing
T-1
testing
T-2
testing
T-2
testing
T-1
testing
T-1
T-2
testing
testing
T-1
T-2
testing
testing
T-2
T-1
```

Solved Examples

```
1 import threading
2 def msg():
3     print('test')
4 t = threading.Thread(target=msg)
5 t.start()
6
7
8
9
```

Output:
```
test
```

```
1 import threading
2 def msg():
3     print('test')
4 for i in range(5):
5     t = threading.Thread(target=msg)
6     t.start()
7
8
9
10
```

Output:
```
test
test
test
test
test
```

```
1 import threading
2 def msg(s):
3     print(s)
4 t = threading.Thread(target=msg,args=('test',))
5 t.start()
6
7
8
9
10
11
12
13
```

Output:
```
test
```

```
1  import threading
   class test(threading.Thread):
3      def __init__(self,name):
4          threading.Thread.__init__(self)
5          self.name=name
6      def run(self):
7          print (self.name)
8  t1=test("t1")
9  t=test("t2")
10 t1.start()
11 t.start()
```

```
1  import threading
   class test():
3      def msg(self):
4          print('test')
5  t=test()
6  t1=threading.Thread(target=t.msg)
7  t1.start()
8
9
```

EXERCISE

1. Set the priorities to the thread.

2. Display all running threads.

3. Print factorial of a number using thread concepts.

4. Print the Fibonacci series using the thread concepts.

5. Program to credit the amount and withdrawal transactions using the semaphore.

## CHAPTER 6

Method Overloading and Operator Overloading

6.1 INTRODUCTION

Overloading is the ability of a function or an operator to behave in different ways based on the parameters that are passed to the function, or the operands that the operator acts on.

There are two types of overloading in Python:

1. Method overloading

2. Operator overloading

The advantages of using the overload are the following:

1. Reusability

2. Improves code clarity and eliminates the complexity

The disadvantages associated with the overloading is the following:

1. Creates confusion and becomes very cumbersome to manage overloaded functions

DOI: 10.1201/9781003462392-6

6.2 METHOD OVERLOADING

Method overloading is the concept of the compile time polymorphism. Method overloading can create a method with the same name and can be called with different arguments. The methods differ with zero, one, or more parameters. Method overloading concept is used in a single class. The method arguments differ in number of arguments and types of arguments.

Program 1: Method overloading with zero and one argument methods

```
class test:
def display(self,s=None):
            if s is not None:
print("one argument method")
else:
print("zero argument method")
t=test()
t.display()
t.display("python")
```

Output

zero argument method
one argument method

In the previous example, the class test defines a method with a single argument having default value, and it is also called without arguments, Python programming language uses these default values while executing the display method. The previous class test contains a method with one argument having default values as None. The default value of None means argument has not been explicitly provided a value. The display method checks the value of these arguments and performs accordingly. An object t of class test is created to call the display method with a single argument. If there is no argument, then display function will return zero argument method, and if we pass one argument to the display method, then it returns the message one argument method.

Program 2: Method overloading with zero, one, and two argument methods

```
class test:
def display(self,a=None,b=None):
if a is None and b is None:
```

```
print("zero argument method")
elif a is not None and b is not None:
print("two argument method")
elif a is not None or b is not None:
print("one argument method")
t=test()
t.display()
t.display("python")
t.display("method","overlaoding")
```

Output

```
zero argument method
one argument method
two argument method
```

In the previous example, the class test defines a display method with two arguments having default value, and it is also called without arguments. Python programming language uses these default values while executing the display method. The previous class test contains a display method with two arguments having default values as None. The display method checks the value of these arguments and performs accordingly. An object t of class test is created to call the display method with two arguments. If there is no argument, then display function will return zero argument method message, and if we pass one argument to the display method, then it returns the message one argument method. If we pass two arguments to the display method, that is, method and overloading parameters, then it returns the message two argument method.

Program 3: Method overloading with different data types

```
class test:
def display(self,datatype,*args):
if datatype=="int":
s=0
elif datatype=="float":
s=0.0
elif datatype=="str":
s=""
for x in args:
s=s+X
print("addition:",s)
```

```
t=test()
t.display("int",1,2,3,4,5)
t.display("float",1.1,2,3)
t.display("str","this","is","to","test") t.display("st
  r","python","3.8")
```

Output

```
addition: 15
addition: 6.1
addition: thisistotest
addition: python3.8
```

In the previous example, variable arguments with different types of arguments are used. The parameter *args accepts the different number of arguments and different types of arguments with using only one display method.

Program 4: Method overloading with same data type but with number of arguments

```
from multiple dispatch import dispatch
@dispatch(int,int)
def sum(a,b):
print(a+b)
@dispatch(int,int,int)
def sum(a,b,c):
print(a+b+c)
@dispatch(int,int,int,int)
def sum(a,b,c,d):
print(a+b+c+d)
@dispatch(int,int,int,int,int)
def sum(a,b,C,d,e):
print(a+b+c+d+e)
sum(1,2)
sum(1,2,3)
sum(1,2,3,4)
sum(1,2,3,4,5)
```

Output

```
3
6
10
15
```

In the preceding program, defined four sum methods as Python supports many methods with the same name and different arguments. The dispatcher stores different implementations during runtime by creating an object for test class and selects the appropriate method as the type and the number of parameters passed.

Program 5: Method overloading with same data type but with number of arguments

```
from multiple dispatch import dispatch
@dispatch(float,float)
def sum(a,b):
print(a+b)
@dispatch(float,float,float)
def sum(a,b,c):
print(a+b+c)
@dispatch(float,float,float,float)
def sum(a,b,c,d):
print(a+b+c+d)
@dispatch(float,float,float,float,float)
def sum(a,b,c,d,e):
print(a+b+c+d+e)
sum(1.1,2.1)
sum(1.4,2.4,3.5)
sum(1.3,2.4,3.5,4.7)
sum(1.0,2.0,3.0,4.0,5.0)
```

Output

```
3.2
7.3
11.9
15.0
```

In the preceding program, defined four sum methods with float data type as the argument as Python supports many methods with similar names and various arguments.

Program 6: Method overloading with same number of parameters but differs with the type of arguments

```
from multiple dispatch import dispatch
@dispatch(int,int,float)
```

```
def sum(a,b,c):
print(a+b+c)
@dispatch(int,float,float)
def sum(a,b,c):
print(a+b+c)
@dispatch(float,int,int)
def sum(a,b,c):
print(a+b+c)
sum(1.1,2,3)
sum(1,2.4,3.5)
sum{1,2,3.5)
```

Output

```
6.1
6.9
6.5
```

In the preceding program, defined four sum methods accepts three arguments and with different data type as the arguments.

6.3 OPERATOR OVERLOADING

The ability to sue the same operator against completely different kinds of data is called operator overloading. The main advantage of using operator overloading is that it is much easier to read and debug. Operators that already exist in the Python language can be overloaded. Operator overloading cannot alter either the basic definition of an operator or the precedence order. The operator overloading can be accomplished by a special function. The general syntax of operator overloading in Python is as follows:

Syntax

```
def __operatormagicword__ (self,object):
#Body of the function
```

Note: Only those operators that are predefined in Python are allowed to be overloaded.

Rules for overloading operators

Rule 1: Only the operators that are predefined in the Python can be used. The programmers cannot create new operators such as $, etc.

Rule 2: The programmers should not change the original meaning of the operator. For example, the operator may be overloaded to multiply the objects of the user-defined class.

Rule 3: The programmers should not change the precedence order or the basic definition of the operator.

6.3.1 Overloading Arithmetic Operators

The special functions that we need to implement the arithmetic operators are given in Table 6.1.

TABLE 6.1   Overloading Arithmetic Operators

S.No	Arithmetic Operator	Special Function
1	+	__add__
2	-	__sub__
3	*	__mul__
4	/	__truediv__
5	//	__floordiv__
6	**	__mod__
7	%	__pow__

Program 7: Python program to add two objects with single argument

```
class test:
def __init__(self,x):
self.x=x
def __add__(self,sample):
x=self.x+sample.x
return test(x)
def __str__(self):
return"{0}".format(self.x)
t1=test(10)
t2=test(20)
print(t1+t2)
```

Output

```
30
```

In the previous example, using binary + operator between the objects t1 and t2 automatically invokes the magic method __add__. The magic method __add__ defined method in the class test and binary operator + work accordingly to the behavior defined in the magic method __add__ and a one int argument is given to the magic method __add__.

Program 8: Python program to add two objects with two arguments

```
class test:
def __init__(self,x,y):
self.x=x
self.y=y
def __add__(self,sample):
x=self.x+sample.x
y=self.y+sample.y
return test(x,y)
def __str__(self):
return"({0},{1})".format(self.x,Self.y)
t1=test(1,2)
t2=test(3,4)
print(t1+t2)
```

Output

```
(4,6)
```

Internally t1+t2 converts to t1. __add__(t2). In the previous example, using binary + operator between the objects t1 and t2 automatically invokes the magic method __add__. The magic method __add__ defined method in the class test and binary operator + work accordingly to the behavior defined in the magic method __add__ and two integer arguments are used in the magic method __add__.

Program 9: Python program to concatenation of strings using operator overloading

```
class test:
def __init__(self,x):
self.x=x
def __add__(self,sample):
x=self.x+sample.x
return test(x)
def __str__(self):
return"{0}".format(self.x)
t1=test("usha")
```

```
t2=test("rani")
print(t1+t2)
```

Output

```
usharani
```

In the previous example, using binary + operator between the objects t1 and t2 automatically invokes the magic method __add__ as works as a concatenation operator as the objects passing the string arguments. The magic method __add__ defined method in the class test and binary operator + work accordingly to the behavior defined in the magic method __add__ and a single string argument is used in the magic method __add__.

Program 10: Python program to add complex numbers using operator overloading

```
class test:
def __init__(self,x,y):
self.x=x
self.y=y
def __add__(self,sample):
x=self.x+sample.x
y=self.y+sample.y
return test(x,y)
def __str__(self):
return"({0}+i{1})".format(self.x,self.y)
t1=test(2,2)
t2=test(3,5)
print(t1+t2)
```

Output

```
(5+i7)
```

In the previous example, using binary + operator between the objects t1 and t2 automatically invokes the magic method __add__ to perform the complex addition.

Program 11: Python program to add object and integer using operator overloading

```
class test:
def __init__(self,x):
```

```
self.x=x
def __add__(self,y):
x=self.x+y
return test(x)
def __str__(self):
return"{0}".format(self.x)
t1=test(10)
print(t1+10)
```

Output

```
20
```

In the previous example, using binary + operator between the object t1 and an integer automatically invokes the magic method __add__ to perform the addition. At the time of creating the object t1, an integer value 10 has been initialized.

Program 12: Python program to add integer and object using operator overloading

```
class test:
class test:
def __init__(self,x):
self.x=x
def __radd__(self,y):
x=self.x+y
return test(x)
def __str__(self):
return"{0}".format(self.x)
t1=test(10)
print(30+t1)
```

Output

```
40
```

In the previous example, using binary + operator between the integer and object t1 automatically invokes the magic method __radd__ to perform the addition.

Program 13: Python program to subtract two objects using operator overloading

```
class test:
def __init__(self,x,y):
self.x=x
self.y=y
def __sub__(self,Sample):
x=self.x-sample.x
y=self.y-sample.y
return test(x,y)
def __str__(self):
return"({0},{1})".format(self.x,Self.y)
t1=test(1,2)
t2=test(3,4)
print(t2-t1)
```

Output

```
(2,2)
```

In the previous example, using binary operator between the objects t1 and t2 automatically invokes the magic method __sub__ as works as a subtraction operator as the objects passing the two integer arguments. The magic method __sub__ defined method in the class test and binary operator work accordingly to the behavior defined in the magic method __sub__ and two integer arguments are used in the magic method __sub__.

Program 14: Python program to multiply two objects using operator overloading with single object argument

```
class test:
def __init__(self,x):
self.x=x
def __mul__(self,sample):
x=self.x*sample.x
return test(x)
def __str__(self):
return"{0}".format(self.x)
t1=test(1)
```

```
t2=test(3)
print(t1*t2)
```

Output

```
3
```

In the previous example, using binary *operator between the objects t1 and t2 automatically invokes the magic method __mul__ as works as a multiplication operator as the objects passing a single integer argument.

Program 15: Multiplication of two objects

```
class test:
def __init__(self,x,y):
self.x=x
self.y=y
def __mul__(self,sample):
x=self.x*sample.x
y=self.y*sample.y
return test(x,y)
def __str__(self):
return"({0},{1})".format(self.x,self.y)
t1=test(1,2)
t2=test(3,4)
print(t1*t2)
```

Output

```
(3,8)
```

In the previous example, using binary *operator between the objects t1 and t2 automatically invokes the magic method __mul__ as works as a multiplication operator as the objects passing two integer arguments.

Program 16: Python program to replicate the string using operator overloading

```
class test:
def __init__(self,x):
self.x=x
def __mul__(self,Sample):
x=self.x*sample.x
```

```
return test(x)
def __str__(self):
return"{0}".format(self.x)
t1=test(3)
t2=test("python")
print(t1*t2)
```

Output

```
pythonpythonpython
```

In the previous example, using binary *operator between the integer and t2 automatically invokes the magic method __mul__ as works as a replication operator.

Program 17: Python program to divide two objects using operator overloading with two arguments in each object

```
class test:
def __init__(self,x,y):
self.x=x
self.y=y
def __truediv__(self,sample):
x=self.x/sample.x y=self.y/sample.y
return test(x,y)
def __str__(self):
return"({0},{1})".format(self.x,self.y)
t1=test(4,8)
t2=test(2,2)
print(t1/t2)
```

Output

```
(2.0,4.0)
```

In the previous example, using binary/operator between the objects t1 and t2 automatically invokes the magic method __truediv__ as works as a division operator as the objects passing the two integer arguments. The magic method __truediv__ defined method in the class test and binary operator/ work accordingly to the behavior defined in the magic method __truediv__ and two integer arguments are used in the magic method __truediv__.

Program 18: Python program to divide two objects (floor division) of two objects using operator overloading

```
class test:
def __init__(self,x,y):
self.x=x
self.y=y
def __floordiv__(self,sample):
x=self.x//sample.x
y=self.y//sample.y
return test(x,y)
def __str__(self):
return"({0},{1})".format(self.x,self.y)
t1=test(4,8)
t2=test(2,2)
print(t1//t2)
```

Output

```
(2,4)
```

In the previous example, using binary // operator between the objects t1 and t2 automatically invokes the magic method __floordiv__as works as a floor division operator as the objects passing the two integer arguments. The magic method __floordiv__ defined method in the class test and binary operator// work accordingly to the behavior defined in the magic method __floordiv__ and two integer arguments are used in the magic method __floordiv__.

6.3.2 Overloading Comparison Operators

To overload the comparison operators in python, the special functions that we need to implement are given in Table 6.2.

TABLE 6.2   Overloading Comparison Operators

S.No	Comparison Operator	Special Function
1	<	__lt__
2	<=	__le__
3	>	__gt__
4	>=	__ge__
5	==	__eq__
6	!=	__ne__

Program 19: Python program to compare two objects (using less than) of two objects using operator overloading with single argument

```
class test:
def __init__(self,x):
self.x=x
def __lt__(self,sample):
return self.x<sample.x
t1=test(2)
t2=test(3)
print(t1<t2)
```

Output

```
True
```

In the previous example, using binary < operator between the objects t1 and t2 automatically invokes the magic method __lt__as works as a less than operator as the objects passing a single integer argument. The magic method __lt__ defined method in the class test and binary operator < work accordingly to the behavior defined in the magic method __lt__ and a single integer argument is used in the magic method __lt__.

Program 20: Python program to compare two objects (using less than) of two objects using operator overloading with two arguments

```
class test:
def __init__(self,X,y):
self.x=x
self.y=y
def __lt__(self,sample):
if self.x<sample.x:
return True
elif self.x==sample.x:
if self.y<sample.x:
return True
else:
return False
else:
return False
t1=test(2,2)
t2=test(3,3)
```

```
print(t1<t2)
t1=test(5,5)
t2=test(5,7)
print(t1<t2)
t1=test(5,5)
t2=test(7,3)
print(t1<t2)
```

Output

```
True
False
True
```

In the previous example, using binary < operator between the objects t1 and t2 automatically invokes the magic method __lt__as works as a less than operator as the objects passing two integer arguments.

Program 21: Python program to compare two objects (using equal to) of two objects using operator overloading with single argument

```
Equality operator overloading
class test:
def __init__(self,x):
self.x=x
def __eq__(self,sample):
return (self.x==sample.x)
t1=test(2)
t2=test(3)
print(t1==t2)
```

Output

```
False
```

In the previous example, using binary comparison =operator between the objects t1 and t2 automatically invokes the magic method __eq__ as works as an equal operator as the objects passing a single integer argument.

Program 22: Python program to compare two objects (using less than) of two objects using operator overloading with single string argument

```
class test:
def __init__(self,x):
```

```
self.x=x
def __eq__(self,sample):
return (self.x==sample.x)
t1=test("python")
t2=test("python")
print(t1==t2)
```

Output

```
True
```

In the previous example, using binary comparison =operator between the objects t1 and t2 automatically invokes the magic method __eq__ as works as an equal operator as the objects passing two integer arguments.

6.3.3 Overloading Assignment Operator

The special functions that we require to execute assignment operators are given in Table 6.3.

TABLE 6.3   Overloading Assignment Operators

S.No	Assignment Operator	Special Function
1	+=	__iadd__
2	-=	__isub__
3	*=	__imul__
4	/=	__idiv__
5	//=	__ifloordiv__
6	%=	__imod__
7	**=	__pow__
8	>>=	__irshift__
9	<<=	__ilshift__
10	&=	__iand__
11	|=	__ior__
12	^=	__ixor__

Program 23: Python program to add two objects (+=) by using the shortcut addition operator with single argument (operator overloading with single argument)

```
class test:
def __init__(self,x):
self.x=x
def __iadd__(self,sample):
```

```
self.x+=sample.x
return test(self.x)
def __str__(self):
return"{0}".format(self.x)
t1=test(3)
t2=test(5)
t1+=t2
print(t1)
```

Output

```
8
```

In the previous example, using shortcut assignment +=operator between the objects t1 and t2 automatically invokes the magic method __iadd__ as works as a shortcut addition operator as the objects passing a single integer argument.

Program 24: Python program to add two objects (+=) by using the shortcut addition operator with two arguments

```
class test:
def __init__(self,x,y):
self.x=x
self.y=y
def __iadd__(self,sample):
self.x+=sample.x
self.y+=sample.y
return test(self.x,self.y)
def __str__(self):
return"({0},{1})".format(self.x,self.y)
t1=test(3,5)
t2=test(5,4)
t1+=t2
print(t1)
```

Output

```
(8,9)
```

In the previous example, using binary assignment +=operator between the objects t1 and t2 automatically invokes the magic method __iadd__ as works as a shortcut addition operator as the objects passing two integer arguments.

Program 25: Python program to add two objects (+=) by using the shortcut addition operator with single two argument and different types.

```
class test:
def __init__(self,x,y):
self.x=x
self.y=y
def __iadd__(self,sample):
self.x+=sample.x
self.y+=sample.y
return test(self.x,self.y)
def __str__(self):
return"({0},{1})".format(self.x,self.y)
t1=test(3,5.1)
t2=test(5.3,4)
t1+=t2
print(t1)
```

Output

```
(8.3,9.1)
```

In the previous example, using binary assignment +=operator between the objects t1 and t2 automatically invokes the magic method __iadd__ as works as a shortcut addition operator as the objects passing three integer arguments.

6.3.4 Overloading Class Operators

The special functions that we need to implement class operators are given in Table 6.4.

TABLE 6.4   Overloading Class Operators

S.No	Class Operator	Special Function
1	getitem()	__getitem__
2	setitem()	_-setitem__
3	delitem()	__delitem__
4	contains ()	__contains__
5	str ()	__str__
6	Call	__call__

Program 26: Overloading [] operator using __getitem__

```
class test:
def __getitem__{self,i):
return i
t=test()
t[1]
```

Output

```
1
```

In the preceding program, the [] operator gets the value at an index, Python manages itr. __getitem__(index), where index is the list index which the user wants to achieve. [] is invoked with a single argument in the previous program.

Program 27: Overloading [] operator using __getitem__

```
class test:
def __init__(self,a):
self.a=list(a)
def __getitem__(self,i):
return self.a[i]
t=test([1,2,3])
t[1]
```

Output

```
2
```

In the preceding program, the [] operator gets the value at an index, Python manages itr. __getitem__(index). [] is invoked with two arguments in the previous program.

Program 28: Overloading [] operator using __getitem__

```
class test:
def __init__(self,a):
self.a=list(a)
def __getitem__(self,i):
return self.a[i]
t=test([1,2,3])
t[-1]
```

Output

```
3
```

In the preceding program, the [] operator gets the value at an index, Python manages itr. __getitem__(index). [] is invoked with a three argument and a negative index in the previous program.

Program 29: Overloading [] operator using __getitem__

```
class test:
def __init__(self,a):
self.a=list(a)
def __getitem__(self,i):
return self.a[i]
t=test([1,2,3])
t[::-1]
```

Output

```
[3, 2, 1]
```

In the preceding program, the [] operator gets the value at an index, Python manages itr. __getitem__(index). [] is invoked with a three argument and a negative index with slicing in the previous program.

Program 30: Overloading [] operator using __getitem__

```
class test:
def __init__(self,a):
self.a=list(a)
def __getitem__(self,i):
return self.a[i]
t=test([1,2,3])
t[1:]
```

Output

```
[2, 3]
```

In the preceding program, the [] operator gets the value at an index, Python manages itr. __getitem__(index). [] is invoked with a three argument and a slicing in the previous program.

Program 31: Overloading [] operator using __setitem__

```
class test:
def __init__(self,a):
self.a=list(a)
def __setitem__(self,index,value):
if len(self.a)>index:
self.a[index]=value
else:
    raise IndexError
def __getitem__(self,i):
return self.a[i]

t=test([1,2,3])
print(t[1:])
t[1]=5
print(t[1:])
```

Output

```
[2, 3]
[5, 3]
```

In the previous program, __setitem__ is used to assign the values. The __setitem__ (self, index, value) assigns the value to the object at the specified index. When the statement t [1] =5 executes, the __setitem__ method is automatically invoked as t1. __setitem__ (5).

Program 32: Overloading [] operator using __delitem__

```
class test:
def __init__(self,a}:
self.a=list(a)
def __getitem__(self,1):
return self.a[i]
def __delitem__(self,index):
del self.a[index]
t=test([1,2,3,4,5])
print(t[0:])
del t[1]
print(t[0:])
```

Output

```
[1, 2, 3, 4, 5]
[1, 3, 4, 5]
```

The __delitem __ (self, index) is used to delete or remove the values at the specified index. The __delitem__ returns the values associated with the key being connected.

Program 33: Overloading __del__

```
class test:
def __init__(self):
print("constructor")
def __del__(self):
print("destructor")
t=test()
del t
```

Output

```
constructor
destructor
```

In the preceding program, __del__ method is invoked when the object of the class is about to get destroyed.

Program 34: Attribute setting using operator overloading

```
class test:
def __init__(self,a):
self.a=a

def __get__(self,*_):
return self.a
def __set__(self,*_):
pass
t=test(10)
print(t.a)
t.a=100
print(t.a)
```

Output

```
10
100
```

In the preceding program, __get__ is used to get the instance of the class, and this method is called with zero or one argument and __set__ method is used to set the instance of the class with a new value.

6.3.5 Overloading the Unary Operators

The special functions that we require to apply unary operators are given in Table 6.5.

TABLE 6.5   Overloading Unary Operators

S.No	Unary Operator	Special Function
1	-	__neg__
2	+	__pos__
3	~	__invert__
4	abs ()	__abs__
5	complex ()	__complex__
6	int ()	__int__
7	float ()	__float__
8	long ()	__long__
9	oct ()	__oct__
10	hex ()	__hex__

Program 35: Python program to perform the negation of the object using the operator overloading

```
class test:
def __init__(self,x):
self.x=x
def __neg__(self):
return test(-self.x)
def __str__(self):
return"({0})".format(self.x)
t1=test(3)
print(-t1)
```

Output

```
(-3)
```

In the preceding program, __neg__ method is used to return the negative value in the test class. Performed the negation on the single value.

Program 36: Python program to get the length of the string argument of the object using the operator overloading

```
class test:
def __init__(self,x):
self.x=list(x)
def __len__(self):
return len(self.x)
t1=[1,2,3,4,5]
print(len(t1))
```

Output

```
5
```

In the preceding program, __len__ method is used to return the length of the list values passed as the argument in the test class.

Program 37: Find the absolute value of the object argument using the operator overloading

```
class test:
def __init__(self,x):
self.x=x
def __abs__(self):
return abs(self.x)
def __str__(self):
return"({0})".format(self.x)
t1=test(-3)
print(abs(t1))
```

Output

```
3
```

In the preceding program, __abs__ method is used to return the absolute value passed as the argument to the __abs__ method in the test class.

Program 38: Python program to perform the negation of the object using the operator overloading with two arguments

```
class test:
def __init__(self,x,y):
self.x=x
self.y=y
def __invert__(self):
x=~self.x
y=~self.y
return test(x,y)
def __str__(self):
return"({0},{1})".format(self.x,self.y)
t1=test(2,2)
print(~t1)
```

Output

```
(-3,-3)
```

In the preceding program, __invert__ method is used to return the negative value in the test class. Performed the negation on the two values.

6.3.6 Overloading of Operators on Lists

The + operator will perform merging on two lists. Some examples for operator overloading on list are given in the next section:

Program 39: Merge two list objects using the operator overloading

```
class test:
def __init__(self,x):
self.x=list(x)
def __add__(self,sample):
x=self.x.copy()
x.append(sample.x)
self.x=x
return test(self.x)
def __str__(self):
return"({0})".format(self.x)
t1=test([2,2])
t2=test([1,5,8])
print(t1+t2)
```

Output

```
([2, 2, [1, 5, 8]])
```

In the preceding example, by using binary + operator between the objects t1 and t2, which consists as the data structure list as the argument automatically invokes the magic method __add__. The magic method __add__ defined method in the class test and binary operator + work accordingly to the behavior defined in the magic method __add__ and an int argument is given to the magic method __add__.

Program 40: Merge the element to the list object utilizing the operator overloading with different argument types

```
class test:
def __init__(self,x):
self.x=list(x)
def __add__(self,sample):
x=self.x.copy()
x.append(sample.x)
self.x=x
return test(self.x)
def __str__(self):
return"({0})".format(self.x)
t1=test([2,2])
t2=test(["usha"])
print(t1+t2)
```

Output

```
([2, 2, ['usha']])
```

In the previous example, by using binary + operator between the objects t1 and t2, which consists as the data structure list as the argument automatically invokes the magic method __add__. The magic method __add__ defined method in the class test and binary operator + work accordingly to the behavior defined in the magic method __add__ and an int argument and the string is given to the magic method __add__.

Program 41: Append the list element to the list object using the operator overloading

```
class test:
```

```
def __init__(self,x):
self.x=list(x)
def __add__(self,s):
x=self.x.copy()
x.append(s)
self.x=x
return test(self.x)
def __str__(self):
return"({0}".format(self.x)
t1=test([2,2])
print(t1+"usharani")
```

Output

```
([2, 2, 'usharani'])
```

In the previous example, by using binary + operator between the objects t1 which consists as the data structure list as the argument and string "usharani" automatically invokes the magic method __add__.

Program 42: Apply the assignment operator on the list object using the operator overloading

```
class test:
def __init__(self,x):
self.x=list(x)
def __iadd__(self,sample):
x=self.x.copy()
x.append(sample.x)
self.x=x
return test(self.x)
def __str__(self):
return"({0})".format(self.x)
t1=test([1,2])
t2=test([3,5,8])
t1+=t2
print(t1)
```

Output

```
([1, 2, [3, 5, 8]])
```

In the previous example, using shortcut assignment +=operator between the objects t1 and t2, which consists as the data structure list as the argument, automatically invokes the magic method __iadd__ as works as a shortcut addition operator as the objects passing an integer argument.

Program 43: Python program to utilize the assignment operator on the list object using the operator overloading

```
class test:
def __init__(self,x):
self.x=list(x)
def __iadd__(self,s):
x=self.x.copy()
x.append(s)
self.x=x
return test(self.x)
def __str__(self):
return"({0})".format(self.x)
t1=test([1,2])
t1+='testing'
print(t1)
```

Output

```
([1, 2, 'testing'])
```

In the previous example, using shortcut assignment +=operator between the objects t1 and t2, which consists as the data structure list as the argument, automatically invokes the magic method __iadd__ as works as a shortcut addition operator as the objects passing an integer argument and a string argument

Program 44: Python program to use the assignment operator on the list object using the operator overloading

```
class test:
def __init__(self,x):
self.x=list(x)
def __iadd__(self,s):
x=self.x.copy()
s=list(s)
x.append(s)
self.x=x
return test(self.x)
def __str__(self):
```

```
return"({0})".format(self.x)
t1=test([1,2])
t1+=[3,4,5]
print(t1)
```

Output

```
([1, 2, [3, 4, 5]])
```

In the previous example, using shortcut assignment +=operator between the objects t1 and t2, which consists as the data structure list as the argument, automatically invokes the magic method __iadd__ as works as a shortcut addition operator as the objects passing an integer argument.

6.3.7 Operator Overloading on Dictionaries

The examples for concatenation of two dictionaries are given in the next section:

Program 45: Python program to merge the element to the dictionary object using the operator overloading

```
class test:
def __init__(self,x):
self.x=dict(x)
def __add__(self,sample):
x=self.x.copy()
x.update(sample.x)
self.x=x
return test(self.x)
def __str__(self):
return"({0})".format(self.x)
t1=test({1:"usha"})
t2=test({2:"rani"})
print(t1+t2)
```

Output

```
({1: 'usha', 2: 'rani'})
```

In the previous example, by using binary + operator between the objects t1 and t2, which consists as the data structure dictionary as the argument, automatically invokes the magic method __add__. The magic method __add__ defined method in the class test and binary operator + work accordingly to the behavior defined in the magic method __add__ and key argument is given to the magic method __add__.

Program 46: Python program to merge the element to the dictionary object using the assignment operator overloading

```
class test:
def __init__(self,x):
self.x=dict(x)
def __iadd__(self,sample):
x=self.x.copy()
x.update(sample.x)
self.x=x
return test(self.x)
def __str__(self):
return"({0})".format(self.x)
t1=test({1:"usha"})
t2=test({2:"rani"})
t3=test({3:"bhimavarapu"})
t1+=t2
t1+=t3
print(t1)
```

Output

```
({1: 'usha', 2: 'rani', 3: 'bhimavarapu'})
```

In the previous example, by using shortcut assignment +=operator between the objects t1, t2, and t3, which consists as the data structure dictionary as the argument, automatically invokes the magic method __iadd__ as works as a shortcut addition operator as the objects passing a key argument.

Program 47: Python program to append the element to the dictionary object using the assignment operator overloading

```
class test:
def __init__(self,x):
self.x=dict(x)
def __iadd__(self,s):
x=self.x.copy()
```

```
s=dict(s)
x.update(s)
self.x=x
return test(self.x)
def __str__(self):
return"({0})".format(self.x)
t1=test({1:"usha"})
t1+=({2:"rani"})
print(t1)
```

Output

```
({1: 'usha', 2: 'rani'})
```

In the previous example, using shortcut assignment +=operator between the objects t1 and t2, which consists as the data structure dictionary as the argument, automatically invokes the magic method __iadd__ as works as a shortcut addition operator as the objects passing a key argument.

Program 48: Python program to merge the element to the dictionary object using the assignment operator overloading

```
class test:
def __init__(self,x):
self.x=dict(x)
def __radd__(self,s):
x=self.x.copy()
s=dict(s)
x.update(s)
self.x=x
return test(self.x)
def __str__(self):
return"({0})".format(self.x)
t1=test({1:"usha"})
print(({2:"rani"})+t1)
```

Output

```
({1: 'usha', 2: 'rani'})
```

In the previous example, using shortcut assignment +=operator between the objects t1 and t2, which consists as the data structure dictionary as the argument, automatically invokes the magic method __radd__ as works as a shortcut addition operator as the objects passing a key argument.

6.4 ELIGIBLE OPERATORS FOR OPERATOR OVERLOADING

The operators that are used for operator overloading are given in Table 6.6.

TABLE 6.6   Overloading Operators

Operator	Method	Operator	Meaning
+	__add__ (self,object)	Binary arithmetic	Binary addition
-	__sub__ (self,object)	Binary arithmetic	Binary subtraction
*	__mul__ (self,object)	Binary arithmetic	multiplication
@	__matmul__ (self,object)	Binary arithmetic	multiplication
//	__floordiv__ (self,object)	Binary arithmetic	Floor division
/	__div__ (self,object)	Binary arithmetic	Integer division
%	__mod__ (self,object)	Binary arithmetic	Modulo
divmod()	__divmod__ (self,object)	Binary arithmetic	Modulo
**	__pow__ (self,object)	Binary arithmetic	Power
<<	__lshift__ (self,object)	Binary bitwise	Left shift
>>	__rshift__ (self,object)	Binary bitwise	Right shift
&	__and__ (self,object)	Binary bitwise	Bitwise and
^	__xor__ (self,object)	Binary bitwise	Bitwise xor
|	__or__ (self,object)	Binary bitwise	Bitwise or
+=	__iadd__ (self,object)	Binary Assignment	Addition assignment
-=	__isub__ (self,object)	Binary Assignment	Subtraction assignment
*=	__imul__ (self,object)	Binary Assignment	Multiplication assignment
/=	__idiv__ (self,object)	Binary Assignment	Division assignment
//=	__ifloordiv__ (self,object)	Binary Assignment	Floor division assignment
%=	__imod__ (self,object)	Binary Assignment	Mod assignment
**=	__ipow__ (self,object)	Binary Assignment	Power assignment
<<=	__ilshift_ (self,object)	Binary Assignment	Left shift assignment
>>=	__irshift__ (self,object)	Binary Assignment	Right shift assignment
&=	__iand__ (self,object)	Binary Assignment	Bit wise and assignment
^=	__ixor__ (self,object)	Binary Assignment	Bit wise xor assignment
|=	__ior__ (self,object)	Binary Assignment	Bit wise or assignment
<	__lt__ (self,object)	Binary Assignment	Less than
>	__gt__ (self,object)	Binary Assignment	Greater than
<=	__le__ (self,object)	Binary Assignment	Less than equal to
>=	__ge__ (self,object)	Binary Assignment	Greater than equal to
==	__eq__ (self,object)	Binary Assignment	Equal to
!=	__ne__ (self,object)	Binary Assignment	Not equal to

(Continued)

TABLE 6.6 (*Continued*) Overloading Operators

Operator	Method	Operator	Meaning
-	__neg__ (self,object)	Unary	Unary minus
+	__pos__ (self,object)	Unary	Unary positive
abs ()	__abs__ (self,object)	Unary	Absolute
~	__invert__ (self,object)	Unary	Negation(or) complement
complex ()	__complex__ (self,object)	Unary	Complex
int ()	__int__ (self,object)	Unary	Integer
long ()	__long__ (self,object)	Unary	Long
float ()	__float__ (self,object)	Unary	Float
oct ()	__oct__ (self,object)	Unary	Octal
hex ()	__hex__ (self,object)	Unary	Hexadecimal
index ()	__index__(self)	Unary	Index
round ()	__round__(self)	Unary	Round
trunc()	__trunc__(self)	Unary	Truncate
floor ()	__floor__(self)	Unary	Floor
ceil ()	__ceil__(self)	Unary	Ceil

EXERCISE

1. Write a Python program to find the absolute of a number using operator overloading.

2. Find the length of the array using operator overloading in Python.

3. Write a Python program to add two hexadecimal numbers using operator overloading.

## CHAPTER 7

GUI Programming

7.1 TKINTER INTERFACE

Python provides many items to develop GUI applications. Out of all these, tkinter is the most commonly used interface. It is the fastest and easiest way to create the GUI applications.

To create the tkinter interface:

1. Import the tkinter module

2. Create the main window

3. Attach the widgets to the main window

4. Apply the event trigger on the widgets

We have to use two main methods to create Python GUI:

```
1.Tk()
```

Syntax

```
Tk(screenName,basename,classname,useTk)
Eg:m=tkinter.Tk();
2.mainloop()- it runs the application
Eg.m.mainloop
We have a give a simple program for GUI application in
  python
```

DOI: 10.1201/9781003462392-7

Program

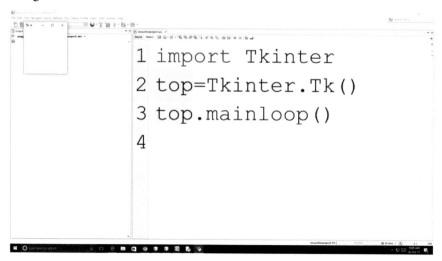

```
1 import Tkinter
2 top=Tkinter.Tk()
3 top.mainloop()
4
```

In the preceding program left side, a window has been opened. It is the tkinter interface.

Program

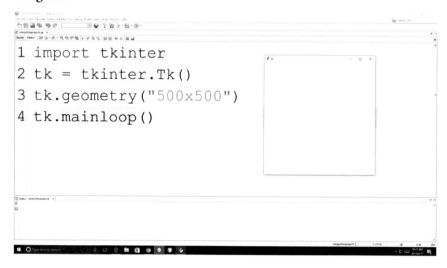

```
1 import tkinter
2 tk = tkinter.Tk()
3 tk.geometry("500x500")
4 tk.mainloop()
```

In the preceding program, interface speciation has been initiated using the geometry method.

7.2 LABEL

Labels are used to place the text or images.

Syntax

```
label=Label()
```

TABLE Label Attributes and Its Description

Option	Description
bg	Background color of the label
bd	Width of the border of the label
font	Font type of the text
fg	Foreground color of the label
height	Height of the label
image	Image shown as the label
padx	Horizontal padding of the text
pady	Vertical padding of the text
text	Text on the label
width	Width of the label

Example 1

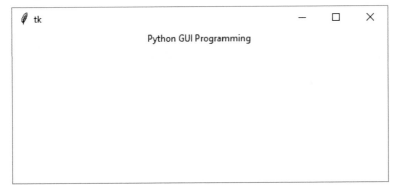

Output

7.3 BUTTON

An action is attached to the button, which happens automatically when the button is clicked.

Syntax

```
Button=Button(master,options);
```

Some options to the button is width, height, padx, pady, justify, etc.

TABLE   Button Attributes and Its Description

Option	Description
activebackground	Background color when the button is highlighted
activeforeground	Foreground color when the button is highlighted
bg	Background color of the button
bd	Width of the border of the button
font	Font type of the text
fg	Foreground color of the button
height	Height of the button
image	Image shown as the button
padx	Horizontal padding of the text
pady	Vertical padding of the text
text	Text on the label
width	Width of the button

TABLE   Button Predefined Methods

Method	Description
flash()	Flashes several times between active and normal colors and ignored if the button is disabled
invoke()	Calls the button's callback and returns that the function returns

Example

```
import tkinter
t=tkinter.Tk()
b=tkinter.Button(t,text ="submit",bg="yellow").pack()
t.geometry("500x200")
t.mainloop()
```

Output

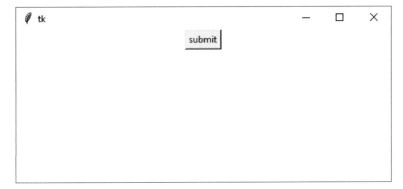

7.4 MESSAGE BOX

The message box widget displays the message boxes on the interface. These message boxes will return values of True, False, OK, Yes, No, None. There are information message boxes, warning message boxes, and question message boxes.

Syntax

```
1.messagebox.showinfo(title,message,**options)
2.messagebox.showwarning(title,message,**options)
3.messagebox.showerror(title,message,**options)
4.messagebox.askokcancel(title,message,**options)
5.messagebox.askquestion(title,message,**options)
6.messagebox.askyesno(title,message,**options)
7.messagebox.askretrycancel(title,message,**options)
```

Output

7.5 MESSAGE

It provides multiline text. The content automatically breaks lines and justify the contents.

Syntax

```
msg=Message(master,option, . . .)
```

TABLE   Message Attributes and Its Description

Option	Description
bg	Background color behind the label
bd	Width of the border around indicator
font	Font type of the text
fg	Text color
height	Height of the frame
image	Image shown in the label
padx	Horizontal padding of the text
pady	Vertical padding of the text
text	Text to be displayed
width	Width of the label in characters

Program

```
import tkinter
from tkinter import Message
t=tkinter.Tk()
label = Message(t,text="Python message exxample",font=("times",36))
label.pack()
t.mainloop()
```

Output

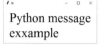

Python message
exxample

Example

```
import tkinter
from tkinter import Message
t=tkinter.Tk()
label = Message(t,text="Python message example",bg='lightpink',bd=15,font=("times",36),relief="solid",width=1000)
label.pack()
t.mainloop()
```

Output

7.6 ENTRY

It accepts single line text from the user.

Syntax

```
E=Entry(master,options, . . .)
```

TABLE   Entry Attributes and Its Description

Option	Description
bg	Background color behind the label
bd	Width of the border around indicator
font	Font type of the text
fg	Text color
highlightcolor	Focus highlight color when cursor is placed in it
selectbackground	Background color to display selected text
show	Text that appears in the entry
xscrollcommand	Link entry to scrollbar
selectforeground	Color of selected text
textvaraible	To retrieve current text from entry
width	Width of the label in characters

TABLE   Entry Predefined Methods

Method	Description
delete(first,last=None)	Deletes characters from first to last index
get()	Returns current text as string
index(index)	Shifts the contents at the given index
insert(index,p)	Inserts string p at the given index
select_to(index)	Selects all the text from pointer to the given index
xview(index)	Links the entry to scrollbar horizontally
select_range(start,end)	Selects the text from start to end index

Example

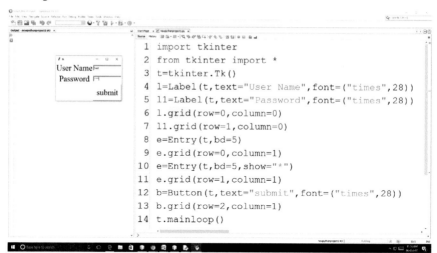

```
1 import tkinter
2 from tkinter import *
3 t=tkinter.Tk()
4 l=Label(t,text="User Name")
5 l.pack(side=LEFT)
6 e=Entry(t,bd=20)
7 e.pack(side=RIGHT)
8 t.mainloop()
```

Example

```
 1 import tkinter
 2 from tkinter import *
 3 t=tkinter.Tk()
 4 l=Label(t,text="User Name",font=("times",28))
 5 l1=Label(t,text="Password",font=("times",28))
 6 l.grid(row=0,column=0)
 7 l1.grid(row=1,column=0)
 8 e=Entry(t,bd=5)
 9 e.grid(row=0,column=1)
10 e=Entry(t,bd=5,show="*")
11 e.grid(row=1,column=1)
12 b=Button(t,text="submit",font=("times",28))
13 b.grid(row=2,column=1)
14 t.mainloop()
```

7.7 CHECKBUTTON

It displays a number of options to the users. The user can select one or more options by clicking the corresponding button.

Syntax

```
Ch=Checkbutton(master,options . . .);
```

TABLE   Checkbutton Attributes and Its Description

Option	Description
bg	Background color behind the label
bd	Width of the border around indicator
font	Font type of the text
fg	Text color
image	Image shown in the label
padx	Horizontal padding of the text
pady	Vertical padding of the text
activebackground	Background color when the button is highlighted
activeforeground	Foreground color when the button is highlighted
disbaledforeground	Foreground color when the button is disabled
width	Width of the label in characters
height	Number of lines of text
Highlightcolor	Color of focus highlight when the button has focus

TABLE   Predefined Methods

Method	Description
flash()	Flashes several times between active and normal colors and ignored if the button is disabled
invoke()	Calls the buttons callback and returns that the function returns
select()	Checks the checkbuton
deselect()	Clears the checkbutton
toggle()	Clears the checkbuttons

Example 1

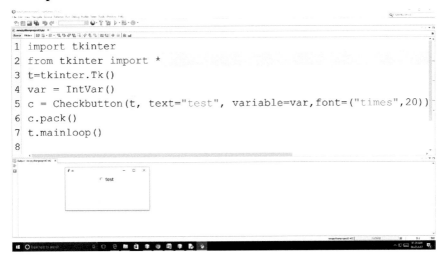

```
1  import tkinter
2  from tkinter import *
3  t=tkinter.Tk()
4  var = IntVar()
5  c = Checkbutton(t, text="test", variable=var,font=("times",20))
6  c.pack()
7  t.mainloop()
8
```

7.8 RADIOBUTTON

It allows the user to choose one of the many options. It contains text or images.

Syntax

```
Rd=Radiobutton(master,options)
```

TABLE   Radiobutton Attributes and Its Description

Option	Description
bg	Background color behind the label
bd	Width of the border around indicator
font	Font type of the text
fg	Text color
image	Image shown in the label
padx	Horizontal padding of the text
pady	Vertical padding of the text
activebackground	Background color when the button is highlighted
activeforeground	Foreground color when the button is highlighted
disbaledforeground	Foreground color when the button is disabled
width	Width of the label in characters
height	Number of lines of text
highlightcolor	Color of focus highlight when the button has focus

TABLE   Predefined Methods

Method	Description
flash()	Flashes radiobutton
invoke()	Calls the button callback and returns that the function returns
select()	Checks the radiobuton
deselect()	Clears the radiobuton

Example

```
1  from tkinter import *
2  from tkinter import messagebox
3  import tkinter
4  t = tkinter.Tk()
5  def test():
6      s=int(v.get())
7      if s==1:
8          s1="u have selected c"
9      elif s==2:
10         s1="u have selected cpp"
11     messagebox.showinfo(" ",s1)
12 v=IntVar()
13 r=Radiobutton(t,text="c",variable=v,value=1,command=test,font=("times",20))
14 r.pack()
15 r1=Radiobutton(t,text="cpp",variable=v,value=2,command=test,font=("times",20))
16 r1.pack()
17 t.mainloop()
```

7.9 LISTBOX

It displays a list of items from which user can select a number of items.

Syntax

```
Lb=Listbox(master,options);
```

TABLE   Listbox Attributes and Its Description

Option	Description
bg	Background color behind the label
bd	Width of the border around indicator
font	Font type of the text
fg	Text color
selectmode	Determines how many items in the listbox can be selected: browse, single, multiple, extended
highlight thickness	Thickness of highlight
selectbackground	Background color to display selected text
xscrollcommand	Scroll the listbox horizontally
yscrollcommand	Scroll the listbox vertically
width	Width of the label in characters
height	Number of lines of text
highlightcolor	Color of focus highlight when the button has focus

TABLE   Listbox Predefined Methods

Method	Description
delete(first,last=None)	Deletes characters from first to last index
get()	Returns current text as string
index(index)	Shifts the contents at the given index
insert(index,p)	Inserts string p at the given index
select_to(index)	Selects all the text from pointer to the given index
xview(index)	Links the entry to scrollbar horizontally
select_range(start,end)	Selects the text from start to end index
nearest(p)	Returns the index of the y coordinate
xview_scroll(number,what)	Scrolls the list horizontally
yview_scroll(number,what)	Scrolls the list vertically

Example 1

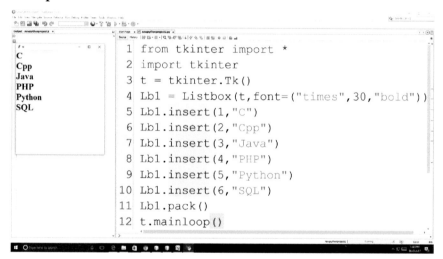

```python
from tkinter import *
import tkinter
t = tkinter.Tk()
Lbl = Listbox(t,font=("times",30,"bold"))
Lbl.insert(1,"C")
Lbl.insert(2,"Cpp")
Lbl.insert(3,"Java")
Lbl.insert(4,"PHP")
Lbl.insert(5,"Python")
Lbl.insert(6,"SQL")
Lbl.pack()
t.mainloop()
```

7.10 SCALE

It provides a graphical slide that allows the user to select values from a specific scale.

Syntax

```
Scale=Scale(master,options, . . .)
```

TABLE   Scale Attributes and Its Description

Option	Description
bg	Background color behind the label
bd	Width of the border around indicator
font	Font type of the text
fg	Text color
activebackground	The background color when the scale is highlighted
highlight background	The color of focus when the scale is not highlighted
selectbackground	Background color to display selected text
from_	Scale range
lenght	Length of the scale
width	Width of the label in characters
repeat delay	How long the button has to be held before the slider starts moving in that direction
slider length	Length of the slider

TABLE   Scale Predefined Methods

Method	Description
set	Set scale value
get()	Returns scale value

Program

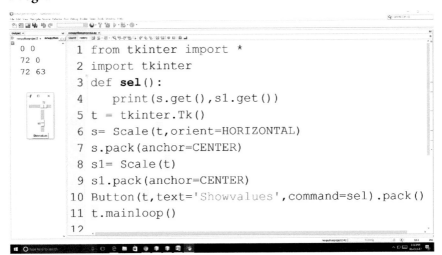

```
 0  0
72  0
72 63
```

```python
1 from tkinter import *
2 import tkinter
3 def sel():
4     print(s.get(),s1.get())
5 t = tkinter.Tk()
6 s= Scale(t,orient=HORIZONTAL)
7 s.pack(anchor=CENTER)
8 s1= Scale(t)
9 s1.pack(anchor=CENTER)
10 Button(t,text='Showvalues',command=sel).pack()
11 t.mainloop()
12
```

```
1  from tkinter import *
2  import tkinter
3  def sel():
4      print(s.get(),s1.get())
5  t = tkinter.Tk()
6  s= Scale(t,orient=HORIZONTAL)
7  s.set(19)
8  s.pack(anchor=CENTER)
9  s1= Scale(t)
10 s1.pack(anchor=CENTER)
11 s1.set(65)
12 Button(t,text='Showvalues',command=sel).pack()
13 t.mainloop()
```

```
1  from tkinter import *
2  import tkinter
3  def sel():
4      print(s.get(),s1.get())
5  t = tkinter.Tk()
6  s= Scale(t,orient=HORIZONTAL,font=("times",30))
7  s.set(19)
8  s.pack(anchor=CENTER)
9  s1= Scale(t,font=("times",30))
10 s1.pack(anchor=CENTER)
11 s1.set(65)
12 Button(t,text='Showvalues',command=sel).pack()
13 t.mainloop()
```

```
1  from tkinter import *
2  import tkinter
3  def sel():
4      print(s.get(),s1.get())
5  t = tkinter.Tk()
6  s1= Scale(t,from_=0,to=42,font=("times",30))
7  s1.pack(anchor=CENTER)
8  s1.set(65)
9  t.mainloop()
10
11
12
13
```

```
from tkinter import *
import tkinter
def sel():
print(s1.get())
t=tkinter.Tk()
s1= Scale(t,from_=0,to=200,tickinterval=10,\
font=("times",18),sliderlength=20)
s1.pack(anchor=CENTER)
Button(t, text='Show',command=sel).pack()
t.mainloop()
```

7.11 SPINBOX

It is used to select a fixed number of values.

Syntax

```
Sb=Spinbox(master,option);
```

TABLE Spinbox Attributes and Its Description

Option	Description
bg	Color of slider
bd	Width of the border around indicator
font	Font type of the text
fg	Text color
activebackground	The background color when the slider is highlighted
format	Format string
xscrollcommand	Horizontal scrollbar
from_	Spinbox range
Repeat interval	Controls autobutton together with repeat delay
width	Width of the label in characters
repeat delay	Controls autobutton
slider length	Length of the slider

TABLE Scale Predefined Methods

Method	Description
delete(start index,end index)	Deletes the range of text
get(start index,end index)	Returns a range of text
identify(a,b)	Identifies elements at the given location
insert(index,[string[, . . .])	Inserts text at specified location

Example 1

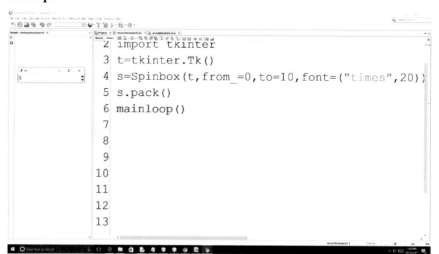

```
2 import tkinter
3 t=tkinter.Tk()
4 s=Spinbox(t,from_=0,to=10,font=("times",20))
5 s.pack()
6 mainloop()
7
8
9
10
11
12
13
```

```
1  from tkinter import *
2  import tkinter
3  t=tkinter.Tk()
4  def sel():
5      print(s.get())
6  s=Spinbox(t,from_=0,to=10,command=sel)
7  s.pack()
8  mainloop()
9
10
```

Example 2

```
1  from tkinter import *
2  import tkinter
3  t=tkinter.Tk()
4  def sel():
5      print(s.get())
6  s=Spinbox(t,values=("c","c++","java"),command=sel)
7  s.pack()
8  mainloop()
9
10
11
12
```

7.12 SCROLLBAR

It provides a slide controller vertically and horizontally on widgets like listbox, spinbox . . .

Syntax:

Sc=Scrollbar(master,options . . .)

TABLE   Scrollbar Attributes

Option	Description
bg	Color of slider
bd	Width of the border around indicator
highlight thickness	Thickness of focus light
highlight	Color of focus when scrollbar has focus
activebackground	The background color when the slider is highlighted
jump	Control when the user drags slider
orient	Horizontal or vertical orientation
takefocus	Tab the focus
repeat interval	Controls autobutton together with repeat delay
width	Width of the label in characters
repeat delay	Controls autobutton
troughcolor	Color of the trough

TABLE   Scrollbar Predefined Methods

Method	Description
get()	Returns the current position of slider
set(first,last)	Sets x scroll command or y scroll command

Example

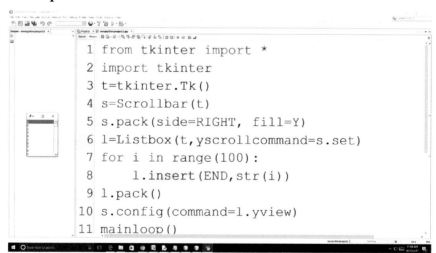

```
1  from tkinter import *
2  import tkinter
3  t=tkinter.Tk()
4  s=Scrollbar(t)
5  s.pack(side=RIGHT, fill=Y)
6  l=Listbox(t,yscrollcommand=s.set)
7  for i in range(100):
8      l.insert(END,str(i))
9  l.pack()
10 s.config(command=l.yview)
11 mainloop()
```

```
1 import tkinter
2 from tkinter import *
3 t=tkinter.Tk()
4 s=Scrollbar(t,orient=HORIZONTAL)
5 s.pack(side=LEFT, fill=X)
6 t.mainloop()
7
```

Example

```
1 import tkinter
2 from tkinter import *
3 t=tkinter.Tk()
4 s=Scrollbar(t,orient=HORIZONTAL)
5 s.pack(fill=BOTH,expand=1)
6 s1=Scrollbar(t,orient=VERTICAL)
7 s1.pack(fill=BOTH,expand=1)
8 t.geometry("300x500")
9 t.mainloop()
```

```
Program using multiple widgets
import sys
import tkinter
from tkinter import *
class popupWindow(object):
def __init__(self,master):
top=self.top=Toplevel(master)
self.l=Label(top,text="wirte some text below")
self.l.pack()
```

```
self.e=Entry(top)
self.e.pack()
self.b=Button(top,text='Ok',command=self.cleanup)
self.b.pack()
def cleanup(self):
self.value=self.e.get()
self.top.destroy()
class mainWindow(object):
def __init__(self,master):
self.master=master
self.b=Button(master,text="click me!",command=self.
  popup)
self.b.pack()
self.b2=Button(master,text="printvalue",command=lambda:
  sys.stdout.write(self.entryValue()+'\n'))
self.b2.pack()
def popup(self):
self.w=popupWindow(self.master)
self.b["state"] = "disabled"
self.master.wait_window(self.w.top)
self.b["state"] = "normal"
def entryValue(self):
return self.w.value
if __name__ == "__main__":
root=tkinter.Tk()
m=mainWindow(root)
root.mainloop()
```

Solved Examples

Example

```
test.py - C:\Users\klu\AppData\Local\Programs\Python\Python36-32\test.py (3.6.2)          —  □  ✕
File  Edit  Format  Run  Options  Window  Help
from tkinter import *
t = Tk()
label = Label( t, borderwidth=5,text="Python GUI Programming",relief="solid")
label.pack()
t.geometry("500x200")
t.mainloop()
                                                                              Ln: 6  Col: 0
```

Output

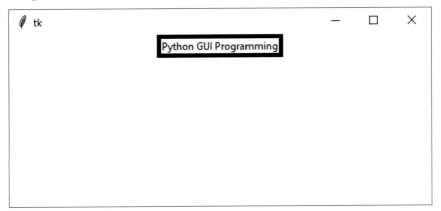

Example

```
from tkinter import *
t = Tk()
l1 = Label( t, borderwidth=5,text="Python GUI Programming",relief="solid")
l1.pack()
l2 = Label( t, borderwidth=5,text="Python GUI Programming",relief="raised")
l2.pack()
l3 = Label( t, borderwidth=5,text="Python GUI Programming",relief="sunken")
l3.pack()
l4 = Label( t, borderwidth=5,text="Python GUI Programming",relief="ridge")
l4.pack()
l5 = Label( t, borderwidth=5,text="Python GUI Programming",relief="groove")
l5.pack()
l6 = Label( t, borderwidth=5,text="Python GUI Programming",relief="flat")
l6.pack()
t.geometry("500x200")
t.mainloop()
```

Output

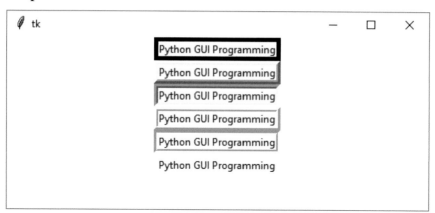

Example

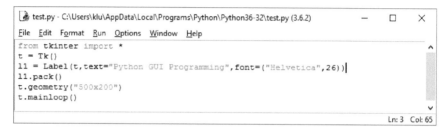

Output

Example

```
from tkinter import *
t = Tk()
l1 = Label(t,text="Python GUI Programming").pack()
t.geometry("500x50")
t.mainloop()
```

Output

Example

Output

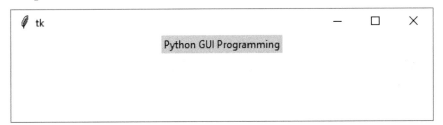

Example

```
import tkinter
t=tkinter.Tk()
b=tkinter.Button(t,text ="submit",bd=15).pack()
t.geometry("500x200")
t.mainloop()
```
Ln: 5 Col: 0

Output

Example

```
test.py - C:\Users\klu\AppData\Local\Programs\Python\Python36-32\test.py (3.6.2)    —    □    ×
File  Edit  Format  Run  Options  Window  Help
import tkinter
from tkinter import messagebox
t=tkinter.Tk()
def test():
    messagebox.showinfo("submit","Button testing")
b=tkinter.Button(t,text ="submit",font=("arial",32),command=test).pack()
t.geometry("500x150")
t.mainloop()
|
                                                                         Ln: 9  Col: 0
```

Output

Example

```
test.py - C:\Users\klu\AppData\Local\Programs\Python\Python36-32\test.py (3.6.2)    —    □    ×
File  Edit  Format  Run  Options  Window  Help
import tkinter
from tkinter import messagebox
t=tkinter.Tk()
def test():
    print("buttonclicked")|
b=tkinter.Button(t,text ="submit",font=("arial",32),command=test).pack()
t.geometry("500x150")
t.mainloop()
                                                                         Ln: 5  Col: 25
```

Output

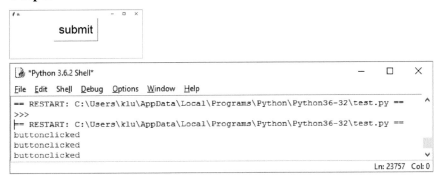

Example

Output

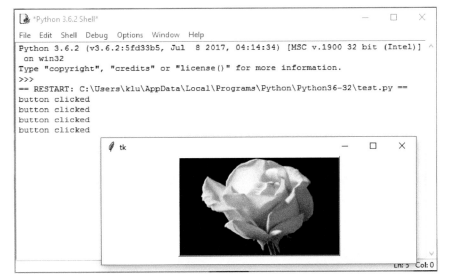

Example 2

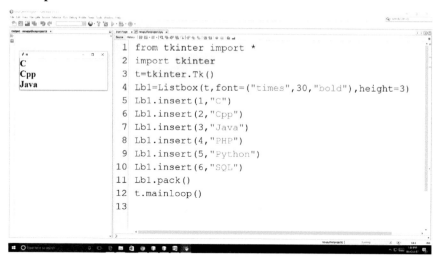

```
1  from tkinter import *
2  import tkinter
3  t=tkinter.Tk()
4  Lbl=Listbox(t,font=("times",30,"bold"),height=3)
5  Lbl.insert(1,"C")
6  Lbl.insert(2,"Cpp")
7  Lbl.insert(3,"Java")
8  Lbl.insert(4,"PHP")
9  Lbl.insert(5,"Python")
10 Lbl.insert(6,"SQL")
11 Lbl.pack()
12 t.mainloop()
13
```

EXERCISE

1. Write a Python program to enter the student details and calculate percentage using widgets.

2. Write a Python program to design a calculator.

3. Write a Python program to design the digital watch.

## CHAPTER 8

File Handling

The variables, lists, tuples, sets, and dictionaries store the data temporarily (volatile). That is, the stored value erases when the program execution completes. To store the data permanently, the file handling plays an important role. A file is a named location on disk to store the information.

The file data is nonvolatile. In Python, files are processed in two modes as text or binary. The file may be in the text or binary format, and each line of a file is concluded with a special character.

Some file operations of Python are as follows:

- Open a file

- Read or write to/from a file

- Close the file

8.1 OPENING A FILE

The Python open () function opens the text file. The open () function accepts two arguments, file name and the access mode in which the file is associated. The function returns a file object that can be utilized to execute various operations like reading, writing, etc.

Syntax

```
File-object=open (fieldname, access-mode, buffering)
```

DOI: 10.1201/9781003462392-8

1. The first parameter specifies the name of the file to be associated with the stream.

2. The second parameter specifies the open mode used for the stream.

3. The third parameter specifies the encoding type.

4. The open file should be the first operation performed on the stream.

5. If the mode string ends with a letter t, the stream is opened in the text mode.

6. If the mode string ends with a letter b, the stream is opened in the binary mode.

7. When no mode specifier is used, the default mode is the text.

The files can be accessed using various modes like read, write, or append. The following table discusses about the access mode to open a file. Various modes and the predefined methods of file are tabulated in Table 8.1 and Table 8.2

TABLE 8.1   Various Modes of File

Access mode	Description
r	Read
rb	Reading only in binary format
r+	Both reading and writing
rb+	Both reading and writing in binary format
w	Write
wb	Writing only in binary format
w+	Both reading and writing
wb+	Both reading and writing in binary format
a	Append
ab	Appending in binary format
a+	Both appending and reading
ab+	Both appending and reading in binary format

TABLE 8.2   Predefined Methods for File Handling

Method	Description
close()	Closes an opened file
detach()	Returns binary buffer from the TextIOBase
fileno()	Returns a number of the file
flush()	Flushes the write buffer
read(n)	Reads at most n characters from the file
readable()	Returns True if the file can be read from
readline(n=-1)	Reads and returns one line from the file
readlines(n=-1)	Reads and returns a list of lines from the file
seek(offset,from=SEEK_SET)	Changes the file position to offset bytes
seekable()	Returns True if the file stream supports random access
tell()	Returns the current file location
truncate(size=None)	Resizes the file stream to size bytes
writable()	Returns True if the file stream can be written to
write(s)	Writes the string s to the file
writelines(lines)	Writes a list of lines to the file

8.2 WRITING TO THE FILES

Syntax

```
File-object=open("filename", "w")
```

Program

```
main.py          test.txt     :
1  f=open("test.txt","w")
2  a=["this is to test\n",
3  "file witelines example\n",
4  "in python and this is\n",
5  "my first example"]
6  f.writelines(a)
7  f.close()
```

```
main.py          test.txt     :
1  this is to test
2  file witelines example
3  in python and this is
4  my first example
```

The preceding program writes multiple lines using wirelines ().

Program

```
main.py        test.txt       ⋮
1  f=open("test.txt","w")
2  f.write("this is to test")
3  f.close()
```

The preceding program writes the contents to the file.

Program

```
main.py        test.txt    ⋮
1  with open('test.txt', 'w') as f:
2          f.write('this is to test')
```

```
main.py        test.txt     ⋮
1  this is to test
```

The preceding program writes content to file using with statement.

Program

```
main.py        test.txt    ⋮
1  f = open('test.txt','w')
2  f.write("this is to test\n")
3  f.write("this is the second line in my file")
4  f.close()
```

```
main.py     test.txt    ⋮
1  this is to test
2  this is the second line in my file
```

The preceding program writes string to a file.

Program

```
main.py        test.txt     ⋮
1  f = open('test.txt', 'w')
2  i = 10
3  f.write(str(i))
4  f.close()
```

```
main.py        test.txt     ⋮
1  10
```

The preceding program writes numbers to a file.

Program

```
main.py        test.txt      ⋮
  1  import pickle
  2  class test(object):
  3      def __init__(self, name):
  4              self.name = name
  5
  6  with open('test.txt', 'wb') as f:
  7
  8      obj1 = test("usha")
  9      pickle.dump(obj1, f, pickle.HIGHEST_PROTOCOL)
 10
 11      obj2 = test("rani")
 12      pickle.dump(obj2, f, pickle.HIGHEST_PROTOCOL)
 13
 14  del obj1
 15  del obj2
 16
 17  with open('test.txt', 'rb') as f1:
 18      obj1 = pickle.load(f1)
 19      print(obj1.name)
 20      obj2 = pickle.load(f1)
 21      print(obj2.name)
```

Output

```
usha
rani
```

The preceding program writes object to file.

Program

```
main.py        test.txt      ⋮
  1  a = ['this', 'is', 'to', 'test']
  2
  3  with open('test.txt', 'w') as f:
  4      for p in a:
  5          f.write('%s\n' % p)
```

Test.txt

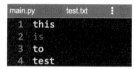

The preceding program writes list data to file.

Program

```
main.py        test.txt    ⋮
1  t = ("this","is","to","test","tuple")
2  f = open("test.txt","w")
3  f.write("".join(t))
4  f.close()
```

```
main.py        test.txt    ⋮
1  thisistotesttuple
```

The preceding program writes tuple data to file.

Program

```
main.py        test.txt    ⋮
1  import pickle
2  s = set(["a", "b", "c"])
3  with open('test.txt','wb') as f:
4      pickle.dump(s, f)
```

The preceding program writes sets to file.

Program

```
main.py        test.txt    ⋮
1  d={'Name' : "usha",
2        'Age' : 31,
3        'Degree' : "P.hD",
4        'University' : "KLEF"}
5
6  with open("test.txt", 'w') as f:
7      for k, v in d.items():
8          f.write('%s:%s\n' % (k, v))
```

```
main.py        test.txt    ⋮
1  Name:usha
2  Age:31
3  Degree:P.hD
4  University:KLEF
```

The preceding program writes dictionary data to file.

Program

```
main.py          test.txt     ⋮
  1  d={'Name' : "usha",
  2         'Age' : 31,
  3         'Degree' : "P.hD",
  4         'University' : "KLEF"}
  5
  6  with open('test.txt','w') as c:
  7      c.write(str(d))
```

```
main.py          test.txt     ⋮
  1  {'Degree': 'P.hD',
  2   'University': 'KLEF',
  3   'Name': 'usha',
  4   'Age': 31}
```

The preceding program writes dictionary data to file.

Program

```python
# Writing to an excel
# sheer using python
import xlwt
from xlwt import Workbook

# Workbook is created
wb = Workbook()

# add_sheet is used to create sheet.
s1 = wb.add_sheet('test1')

s1.write(1, 0, 'this')
s1.write(2, 0, 'is')
s1.write(3, 0, 'to')
s1.write(4, 0, 'test')
s1.write(5, 0, 'excel')
s1.write(0, 1, 10)
s1.write(0, 2, 20)
s1.write(0, 3, 30)
s1.write(0, 4, 40)
s1.write(0, 5, 50)

wb.save('test.xls')
```

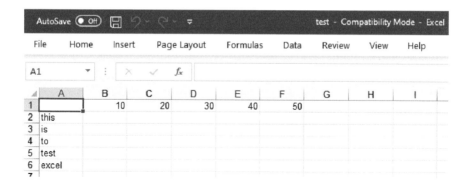

The preceding program writes data to excel file.

Program

```
import xlrd

# Define the location of the file
p = ("test.xls")

# To open the Workbook
wb = xlrd.open_workbook(p)
s = wb.sheet_by_index(0)
```

```
# For row 0 and column 0
s.cell_value(0, 5)
```

```
50.0
```

Th preceding program retrieves the value at a specific cell from the excel file.

8.2.1 Reading the Files

Syntax

```
File-object=open ("filename", "r")
```

Program

```
main.py        test.txt    ⋮
1  f=open("test.txt","r")
2  print(f.read())
```

```
main.py        test.txt    ⋮
1  this is to test
```

Output

```
this is to test
```

The preceding program reads contents of the file.

8.2.2 Readlines

The readline () method reads the lines of the file from the starting of the line.

Program

```
main.py        test.txt    ⋮
1  with open("test.txt") as f:
2      d=f.readlines()
3      for line in d:
4          w=line.split()
5          print(w)
```

```
main.py        test.txt    ⋮
1  this is to test
2  this is file example
3  this is to test the file in pyhton
4  this is a simple example for readlines
```

Output

```
['this', 'is', 'to', 'test']
['this', 'is', 'file', 'example']
['this', 'is', 'to', 'test', 'the', 'file', 'in', 'pyhton']
['this', 'is', 'a', 'simple', 'example', 'for', 'readlines']
[]
[]
[]
[]
[]
```

The preceding program reads multiple lines from file.

Program

```
main.py          test.txt       ⋮
1  with open("test.txt") as f:
2       print("f.read(1):",f.read(1))
3       print("f.read(5):",f.read(5))
4       print("f.read(25):",f.read(25))
5       print("f.read(100):",f.read(100))
```

```
main.py          test.txt       ⋮
1  this is to test
2  this is file example
3  this is to test the file in pyhton
4  this is a simple example for readlines
```

Output

```
f.read(1): t
f.read(5): his i
f.read(25): s to test
this is file ex
f.read(100): ample
this is to test the file in pyhton
this is a simple example for readlines
```

The preceding program reads file content using read ().

Program

```
main.py          test.txt       ⋮
1  with open("test.txt") as f:
2       print(f.read())
3
```

```
main.py          test.txt       ⋮
1  this is to test
```

Output

```
this is to test
```

The preceding program reads file contents using with statement.

Program: Number read

```
main.py          test.txt    ⋮
1  f = open('test.txt', 'r')
2  content = f.readlines()
3  for line in content:
4      for i in line:
5          if i.isdigit() == True:
6              print(i)
```

```
main.py        test.txt      ⋮
1  this 1 test 4 sum
```

Output

Program: Reading list data from file

```
main.py        test.txt    ⋮
1  a = []
2  with open('test.txt', 'r') as f:
3      for i in f:
4          t = i[:-1]
5          a.append(t)
6  print(a)
```

```
main.py        test.txt      ⋮
1  this is to test
```

Output

```
['this is to test']
```

The preceding program reads the file content and stored in the list.

Program

```
main.py        test.txt    ⋮
1  a = []
2
3  with open('test.txt', 'r') as f:
4      for p in f:
5          s = p[:-1]
6          a.append(s)
7  print(a)
```

```
main.py        test.txt    ⋮
 1  this
 2  is
 3  file
 4  list
 5  example
```

Output

```
['this ', 'is ', 'file', 'list', 'example', '', '']
```

The preceding program reads data from file using loops.

Program

```
main.py        test.txt    ⋮
 1  import re
 2  p='\((\d+,\d)\)'
 3  with open('test.txt','r') as f:
 4      for m in f:
 5          n=re.findall(p,m)
 6          r=[tuple(map(lambda x:int(x),
 7                      m.split(','))) for m in n]
 8          if r:
 9              print(r)
```

```
main.py        test.txt    ⋮
 1  (0,0) (0,0) (1,0) (2,3)
 2  (1,0) (1,1) (1,1) (3,3)
 3  (2,0) (1,2) (2,1) (4,4)
 4  (3,0) (2,2) (3,1) (5,5)
```

Output

```
[(0, 0), (0, 0), (1, 0), (2, 3)]
[(1, 0), (1, 1), (1, 1), (3, 3)]
[(2, 0), (1, 2), (2, 1), (4, 4)]
[(3, 0), (2, 2), (3, 1), (5, 5)]
```

The preceding program reads tuple data from file.

Program

```
main.py        test.txt    ⋮
 1  import pickle
 2  with open('test.txt','rb') as f:
 3      my_set = pickle.load(f)
 4  print(my_set)
```

Output

```
{'a', 'b', 'c'}
```

The preceding program reads sets from file.

Program

```
main.py          test.txt        ⋮
1  import ast
2  f = open("test.txt", "r")
3
4  c = f.read()
5  d = ast.literal_eval(c)
6
7  f.close()
8
9  print(d)
```

```
main.py          test.txt        ⋮
1  {'a': 100, 'b': 200}
```

Output

```
{'b': 200, 'a': 100}
```

The preceding program reads dictionary data from file.

Program

```
main.py          test.txt        ⋮
1  with open("test.txt") as f:
2      print(f.readlines())
```

The preceding program reads file content using readlines ().

8.3 THE CLOSE () METHOD

Syntax

```
fileobject.close()
```

Program: Close () method

```
main.py          test.txt        ⋮
1  f = open("test.txt", "r")
2  print( "Name of the file: ", f.name)
3  f.close()
```

Output

```
Name of the file:  test.txt
```

8.4 WITH STATEMENT

The with statement is useful in case of modifying the contents of the files.

Syntax

```
with open (file name, access mode) as file pointer:
```

Program

```
1  with open("test.txt","r") as f:
2      print(f.read())
```
```
this is to test
```

The preceding program reads file content using with statement.

Program

```
1  with open("test.txt") as f:
2      for line in f:
3          print(line)
```

Output

```
this is to test

this is file example

this is to test the file in pyhton

this is a simple example for readlines
```

8.5 APPENDING TO THE FILES

Python can append the content to the already existing file.

Program

```
main.py        test.txt      ⋮
1  this is to test
```

```
main.py      test.txt     ⋮
1 ∙ with open("test.txt","a") as f:
2        f.write("this is an appended line")
```

```
main.py       test.txt     ⋮
1  this is to test
2  this is an appended line
```

The preceding program appends content to already existing file using with statement.

Program

```
main.py        test.txt      ⋮
1  this is to test
```

```
main.py       test.txt      ⋮
1  f=open("test.txt","a")
2  print(f.write("this is appended text"))
```

Output

```
21
```

The preceding program prints the file size of the appended user-defined file.

8.6 FILE POINTER POSITIONS

Python offers the tell () method, which is exploited to print the byte number at which the file pointer currently exists.

Program: Using tell ()

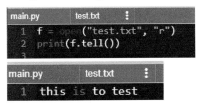

```
main.py        test.txt      ⋮
1  f = open("test.txt", "r")
2  print(f.tell())
3
```

```
main.py        test.txt      ⋮
1  this is to test
```

Output

```
main.py          test.txt    ⋮   sample.txt   ⋮
1  import os
2  os.rename("test.txt","sample.txt")
0
```

Program

```
main.py          test.txt    ⋮
1  this is to test
```

```
main.py          test.txt    ⋮
1  f = open("test.txt", "r")
2  print(f.readline())
3  print(f.tell())
```

Output

```
this is to test

16
```

8.6.1 Modifying File Pointer Position

Python provides the seek () method to alter the file pointer position externally.

Syntax

```
Fileobject.seek(offset,from)
```

Program: Using seek ()

```
Parameters:
offset
from:
```

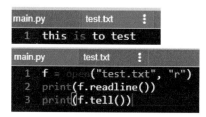

```
main.py          test.txt    ⋮
1  f = open("test.txt", "r")
2  print(f.seek(4))
3  print(f.readline())
```

```
main.py          test.txt    ⋮
1  this is to test
```

```
4
is to test
```

```python
with open("test.txt") as f:

    print("f.read(1):",f.read(1))
    f.seek(0)
    print("f.read(5):",f.read(5))
    f.seek(0)
    print("f.read(25):",f.read(25))
    f.seek(0)
    print("f.read(100):",f.read(100))
```

```
this is to test
this is file example
this is to test the file in pyhton
this is a simple example for readlines
```

Output

```
f.read(1): t
f.read(5): this
f.read(25): this is to test
this is f
f.read(100): this is to test
this is file example
this is to test the file in pyhton
this is a simple example for
```

Program

```python
with open("test.txt") as f:

    print("f.read(1):",f.read(1))
    print("Cursor at:",f.tell())
    f.seek(0)
    print("f.read(5):",f.read(5))
    print("Cursor at:",f.tell())
    f.seek(0)
    print("f.read(25):",f.read(25))
    print("Cursor at:",f.tell())
    f.seek(0)
    print("f.read(100):",f.read(100))
    print("Cursor at:",f.tell())
```

```
f.read(1): t
Cursor at: 1
f.read(5): this
Cursor at: 5
f.read(25): this is to test
this is f
Cursor at: 26
f.read(100): this is to test
this is file example
this is to test the file in pyhton
this is a simple example for
Cursor at: 103
```

The preceding program uses the tell and the seek methods to display and set the current file location.

8.6.2 Renaming the File

Python provides the rename () method to rename the specified file to a new name.

Syntax

```
rename(oldname,new name)
```

Program

```
main.py        test.txt    ⋮  sample.txt  ⋮
1  import os
2  os.rename('test.txt','sample.txt')
```

```
main.py        test.txt    ⋮  sample.txt  ⋮
1  this is to test
```

```
main.py        test.txt    ⋮  sample.txt  ⋮
1  this is to test
```

Program

8.7 BINARY FILE

Program

```
main.py        test.txt    ⋮
1  f=open("test.txt","wb")
2  f.write(b"this is to test a sample")
```

Output

```
main.py        test.txt      ⋮
  1  this is to test a sample
```

The preceding program writes the contents to the user-defined file using binary mode.

Program

```
main.py        test.txt      ⋮
  1  import numpy as np
  2  np.savetxt("test.txt", np.array([[1, 2], [3, 4]]), fmt="%s")
```

```
main.py        test.txt      ⋮
  1  1 2
  2  3 4
```

The preceding program writes the **byte array** data in the binary file.

Program

```
main.py        test.txt      ⋮
  1  f=open("test.txt","rb")
  2  print(f.read())
```

Output

```
b'this is to test\r\n\r\n'
```

The preceding program reads the file contents in the binary mode.

Program

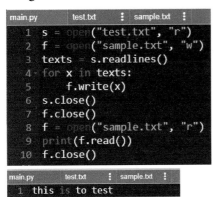

```
main.py        test.txt      ⋮   sample.txt   ⋮
  1  s = open("test.txt", "r")
  2  f = open("sample.txt", "w")
  3  texts = s.readlines()
  4  for x in texts:
  5      f.write(x)
  6  s.close()
  7  f.close()
  8  f = open("sample.txt", "r")
  9  print(f.read())
 10  f.close()
```

```
main.py        test.txt      ⋮   sample.txt   ⋮
  1  this is to test
```

Output

`this is to test`

The preceding program copies the contents of one file to another file.

8.8 RANDOM ACCESS FILES

Program: Random access file

```
main.py          test.txt       ⋮
1  f=open("test.txt","w")
2  f.write("this is to test")
3  f.seek(0,0)
4  f.write("example")
5  f.seek(0,2)
6  f.write("python file example")
7  f.seek(0,1)
8  f.write("sample")
```

```
main.py          test.txt       ⋮
1  example to testpython file examplesample
```

EXERCISE

1. Program to print the first five lines of the file.

2. Program to print last five lines of the file.

3. Extract the numbers form the file and store it in array.

4. Extract the numbers form the file and calculate the sum of those numbers.

5. Count the number of lines of the file.

6. Print the frequent occurrences of the word in the file.

7. Remove the non-alpha characters from the file.

8. Sort the contents of the file in lexicographic order.

## CHAPTER 9

Database Connectivity

A database connection allows client software to connect to the database server. A connection is required to send or receive commands to the database. The Python programs can access the MYSQL and Oracle database. The users can connect and run queries for MYSQL or Oracle using python. To communicate to the database, the users have to install the specific database system in their computer. Later the users verify the their Python version is supporting the MYSQLdb. Figure 9.1 shows the MYSQL driver in the Python shell.

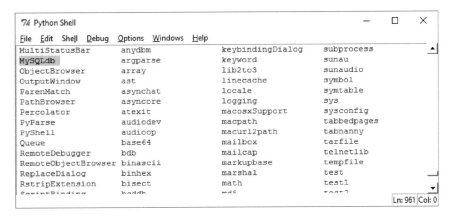

FIGURE 9.1 MYSQLdb in Python shell.

DOI: 10.1201/9781003462392-9

9.1 PYTHON WITH MYSQL

Steps to connect the Python application to the database:

1. Import mysql.connector module

2. Create the object for the connection class to establish the connection between the Python program and Oracle database

3. Create the object for the cursor class to execute the query

4. Execute the user-specified query

Figure 9.2 shows the overall architecture of the Python program interaction with MYSQL database.

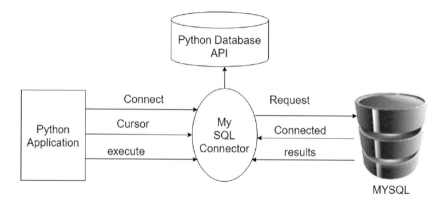

FIGURE 9.2 MYSQL database connection with MYSQL.

Syntax for connecting to database

```
db=mySQLdb.connect("localhost","username","password","
  databasenameinmysql")
```

Sample database program

```
1 import MySQLdb
2 db = MySQLdb.connect("localhost","root","python","test")
3 cursor = db.cursor()
4 cursor.execute("SELECT VERSION()")
5 data = cursor.fetchone()
6 print "Database version : %s " % data
7 db.close()
8
```

```
Database version : 5.5.16
```

The connect () method in the MYSQL module creates the connection between MYSQL and the Python program. In the preceding program, the parameters to the connect method are the hostname and username, password of the MYSQL database. The cursor () allows the user to perform multiple operations row by row against the result set. In the previous section we are printing the MYSQL database version.

9.2 PYTHON WITH ORACLE

The Python programs can access the data of the Oracle database. To communicate to the Oracle database the users have to the install the Oracle database system in their computer. Later the users verify the their Python version is supporting the Oracle driver. Figure 9.3 shows the Oracle driver in the Python shell.

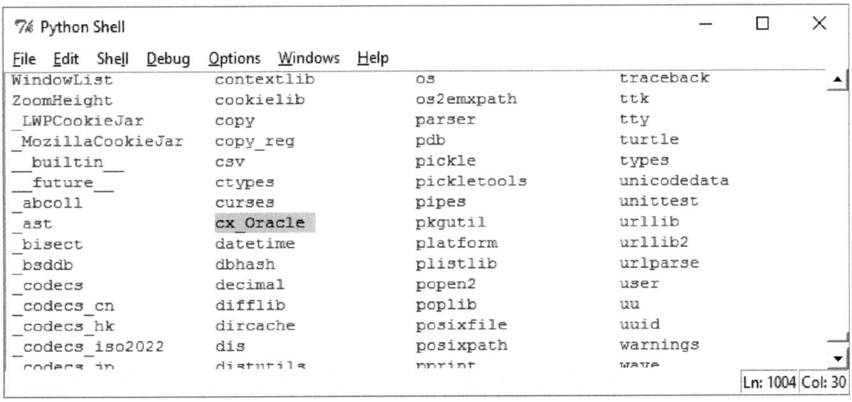

FIGURE 9.3 Oracle driver.

Steps to connect the Python application to the Oracle database:

1. Import cx_Oracle module

2. Create the object for the connection class to establish the connection between the Python program and Oracle database

3. Create the object for the cursor class to execute the query

4. Execute the user-specified query

Syntax

```
connection = cx_Oracle.connect('userid/password@
   hostname:PORT/SID')
```

Figure 9.4 shows the overall architecture of the python program interaction with Oracle database

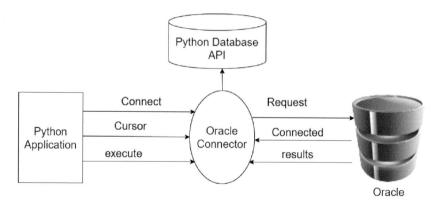

FIGURE 9.4 Oracle database connection with MYSQL.

Program: Printing the version of the Oracle

```
import cx_Oracle
con = cx_Oracle.connect('system/python')
print(con.version)
con.close()
```

Output

10.2.0.1.0

The connect () method in the cx_Oracle module creates the connection between Oracle and the Python program. In the preceding program the parameters to the connect method are the hostname and username, password of the MYSQL database. In the previous section, we are printing the Oracle database version.

Solved Examples

Program: Retrieving the data from the Oracle database

```
import cx_Oracle
con = cx_Oracle.connect('system/python@localhost')
cur = con.cursor()
cur.execute('select*from test')
res = cur.fetchall()
for r in res:
print(r)
cur.close()
con.close()
```

Output

```
(1,)
(2,)
(3,)
(4,)
(5,)
```

Program: Display table data from MYSQL

```
1 import MySQLdb
2 db = MySQLdb.connect("localhost","root","python","mysql")
3 cursor = db.cursor()
4 cursor.execute("SELECT *from test")
5 data = cursor.fetchall()
6 for row in data:
7     print row[0]
8 db.close()
```

```
10
15
25
```

Program: Create table in MYSQL

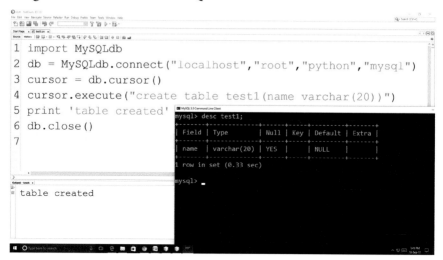

```python
1 import MySQLdb
2 db = MySQLdb.connect("localhost","root","python","mysql")
3 cursor = db.cursor()
4 cursor.execute("create table test1(name varchar(20))")
5 print 'table created'
6 db.close()
7
```

```
mysql> desc test1;
+-------+-------------+------+-----+---------+-------+
| Field | Type        | Null | Key | Default | Extra |
+-------+-------------+------+-----+---------+-------+
| name  | varchar(20) | YES  |     | NULL    |       |
+-------+-------------+------+-----+---------+-------+
1 row in set (0.33 sec)

mysql>
```

```
table created
```

Program: Insert rows in MYSQL

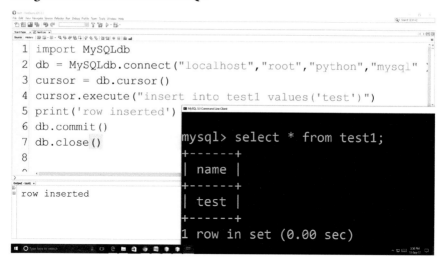

```python
1 import MySQLdb
2 db = MySQLdb.connect("localhost","root","python","mysql"
3 cursor = db.cursor()
4 cursor.execute("insert into test1 values('test')")
5 print('row inserted')
6 db.commit()
7 db.close()
8
```

```
mysql> select * from test1;
+------+
| name |
+------+
| test |
+------+
1 row in set (0.00 sec)
```

```
row inserted
```

Program: Delete data from MYSQL

```
1  import MySQLdb
2  db = MySQLdb.connect("localhost","root","python","mysql" )
3  cursor = db.cursor()
4  cursor.execute("delete from test1 where name='test'")
5  print('row deleted')
6  db.commit()
7  db.close()
8
```

```
mysql> select * from test1;
Empty set (0.00 sec)

mysql>
```

row deleted

Program: Update data in MYSQL

```
1  import MySQLdb
2  db = MySQLdb.connect("localhost","root","python","mysql" )
3  cursor = db.cursor()
4  cursor.execute("update test1 set name='hi' where name='test'")
5  print('row updated')
6  db.commit()
7  db.close()
8
9
```

```
mysql> select * from test1;
+------+
| name |
+------+
| hi   |
+------+
1 row in set (0.00 sec)
```

row updated

Program: Prepared statement in MYSQL

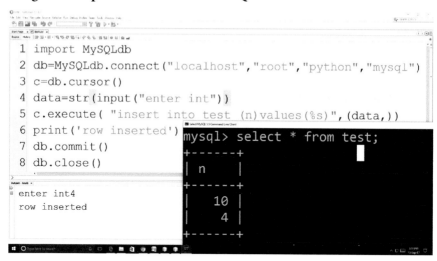

```
1 import MySQLdb
2 db=MySQLdb.connect("localhost","root","python","mysql")
3 c=db.cursor()
4 data=str(input("enter int"))
5 c.execute( "insert into test (n)values(%s)",(data,))
6 print('row inserted')
7 db.commit()
8 db.close()
```

```
enter int4
row inserted
```

```
mysql> select * from test;
+------+
| n    |
+------+
|   10 |
|    4 |
+------+
```

Program: Stored procedure without parameters

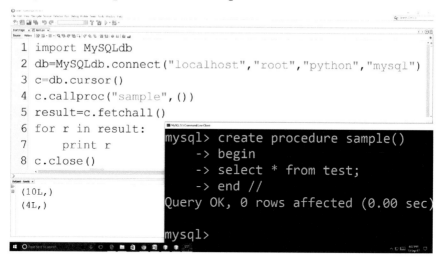

```
1 import MySQLdb
2 db=MySQLdb.connect("localhost","root","python","mysql")
3 c=db.cursor()
4 c.callproc("sample",())
5 result=c.fetchall()
6 for r in result:
7     print r
8 c.close()
```

```
(10L,)
(4L,)
```

```
mysql> create procedure sample()
    -> begin
    -> select * from test;
    -> end //
Query OK, 0 rows affected (0.00 sec)

mysql>
```

Program: Stored procedure with parameters

```
1 import MySQLdb
2 db=MySQLdb.connect("localhost","root","python","mysql")
3 c=db.cursor()
4 r=c.callproc("sq",(10,0))
5 c.execute('SELECT @_sq_1')
6 r=c.fetchone()
7 print(r)
8 c.close()
```

```
(100L,)
```

```
mysql> delimiter //
mysql> create procedure sq(in n1 int,out n2 int)
    -> begin
    -> set n2:=n1 * n1;
    -> end //
Query OK, 0 rows affected (0.00 sec)

mysql> delimiter ;
```

Program: Retrieving the data from the Oracle database

```
import cx_Oracle
uid="system"
pwd="python"
service="localhost"
db = cx_Oracle.connect(uid + "/" + pwd + "@"+ service)
cursor = db.cursor()
cursor.execute("select * from test")
rows = cursor.fetchall()
print ("#-records:", cursor.rowcount)
for i in range(0, cursor.rowcount):
print (rows[i])
cursor.close()
```

Output

```
#-records: 5
(1,)
(2,)
(3,)
(4,)
(5,)
```

Program: Inserting rows to the Oracle database

```
import cx_Oracle
con = cx_Oracle.connect('system/python@localhost')
rows = [(1,"one"), (2,"two"), (3,"three"), (4,"four"),
  (5,"five"), (6,"six"), (7,"seven"), (8,"eight")]
cur = con.cursor()
cur.executemany("insert into test1(id, data) values
  (:1, :2)", rows)
con.commit()
cur2 = con.cursor()
cur2.execute('select * from test1')
res = cur2.fetchall()
for row in res:
print(row)
cur.close()
cur2.close()
con.close()
```

Output

```
(1, 'one')
(2, 'two')
(3, 'three')
(4, 'four')
(5, 'five')
(6, 'six')
(7, 'seven')
(8, 'eight')
```

Program: Prepared statement when more than one value in Oracle

```
import cx_Oracle
con = cx_Oracle.connect('system/python@localhost')
```

```
cur = con.cursor()
row=[]
val=raw_input("enter integer")
val1=raw_input("enter string")
r=(val,val1)
row.append(r)
cur.prepare("INSERT INTO test1 (id,data) VALUES
  (:1,:2)")
cur.executemany(None,row)
con.commit()
cur.close()
con.close()
```

Output

EXERCISE

1. Create the bakery table (id, item, cost, weight) in MYSQL and insert rows in that table using Python program.

2. Update the cost in the previous step and create bakery table using Python program.

3. Create the student table (ID, sname, branch, percentage) in Oracle database and insert rows in that table using Python program.

4. Fetch all the computer students from the previous step and create student table using Python program.

## CHAPTER 10

Case Study

This chapter discusses different case studies uisng Python.

10.1 PROGRAM 1: WHATS APP ANALYSER

This program gives the feature of retreving the chat information from different users and also from different devices.

Step 1: Import all the required libraries and modules.

```
import re
import regex
import pandas as pd
import numpy as np
import emoji
import plotly.express as px
from collections import Counter
import matplotlib.pyplot as plt
from os import path
```

Step 2: The definition starts with data and time android () extracts all the chat file by using the library regex.

```
s
def startsWithDateAndTimeAndroid(s):
pattern = '^([0-9]+)(\/)([0-9]+)(\/)([0-9]+), ([0-
  9]+):([0-9]+) []?(AM|PM|am|pm)? -'
```

DOI: 10.1201/9781003462392-10

```
result = re.match(pattern, s)
if result:
return True
return False
```

Step 3: The method find author () detects the author by identtifying the new messages with data and time components. In this method also regular expression matching is used.

```
def FindAuthor(s):
s=s.split(":")
if len(s)==2:
return True
else:
return False
```

Step 4: The method get data point android () extracts the data from the android, which was identified by the date, time, author, and the message. Splits the each line based on the tokens like commas, hyphens, colons, and spaces. The author information and the data information are stored in the data frames.

```
def getDataPointAndroid(line):
splitLine = line.split(' - ')
dateTime = splitLine[0]
date, time = dateTime.split(', ')
message = ' '.join(splitLine[1:])
if FindAuthor(message):
splitMessage = message.split(':')
author = splitMessage[0]
message = ' '.join(splitMessage[1:])
else:
author = None
return date, time, author, message
```

Step 5: The method get data point android () extracts the data from the IOS, which was identified by the date, time, author, and the message. Splits each line based on the tokens like commas, hyphens, colons, and spaces. The author information and the data information are stored in the data frames.

```
def getDataPointios(line):
splitLine = line.split('] ')
```

```
dateTime = splitLine[0]
if ',' in dateTime:
date, time = dateTime.split(',')
else:
date, time = dateTime.split(' ')
message = ' '.join(splitLine[1:])
```

Step 6: Calling the find author () method, which detects the author-based messages. If there exists special author, then that author's message will be retreived. After retreving the specific author's information, the information will be processed. Splits each line based on the tokens.

```
if FindAuthor(message):
splitMessage = message.split(':')
author = splitMessage[0]
message = ' '.join(splitMessage[1:])
else:
author = None
if time[5]==":":
time = time[:5]+time[-3:]
else:
if 'AM' in time or 'PM' in time:
time = time[:6]+time[-3:]
else:
time = time[:6]
return date, time, author, message
```

Step 7: The method split count () detects the emoijis in the messages.

```
def split_count(text):
emoji_list = []
data = regex.findall(r'\X', text)
for word in data:
if any(char in emoji.UNICODE_EMOJI for char in word):
emoji_list.append(word)

return emoji_list
```

Step 8: Parsing the data and handles the messages that existed on multiple line and also the mutliple messages from the same user and also from the different users.

```
parsedData = [] `'
conversationPath = data.txt'
with open(conversationPath, encoding="utf-8") as fp:
device=''
first=fp.readline()
print(first)
if `[' in first:
device=`ios'
else:
device="android"
fp.readline()
messageBuffer = []
date, time, author = None, None, None
```

Step 9: Parsing the data and handles the messages from different device platforms.

```
while True:
line = fp.readline()
if not line:
break
if device=="ios":
line = line.strip()
if startsWithDateAndTimeios(line):
if len(messageBuffer) > 0:
parsedData.append ([date, time, author, '
  `.join(messageBuffer)])
messageBuffer.clear()
date, time, author, message = getDataPointios(line)
  messageBuffer.append(message)
else:
line= (line.encode('ascii', 'ignore')).decode("utf-8")
if startsWithDateAndTimeios(line):
if len(messageBuffer) > 0:
parsedData.append([date, time, author, `
  '.join(messageBuffer)])
messageBuffer.clear()
date, time, author, message = getDataPointios(line)
```

```
messageBuffer.append(message)
else:
messageBuffer.append(line)
```

Step 10: Processing the data by removing the null values from the data set.

```
df = df.dropna() #drops all null values
```

Step 11: Extracts all the chat file by using the library regex.

```
URLPATTERN = r '(https?://\S+)' #regex pattern
  matching with start with https
df['urlcount'] = df.Message.apply(lambda x:
re.findall(URLPATTERN, x)).str.len()
links = np.sum(df.urlcount) #sumup all the links
print(links)
```

Step 12: Prints the different author messages, the count of the messages sent by a single author, and the average number of the words of the message for each user.

```
frnds = messages_df.Author.unique()
for i in range(len(frnds)):
# Filtering out messages of particular user
req_df= messages_df[messages_df["Author"] == frnds[i]]
# req_df will contain messages of only one particular
  user print(f'Stats of {frnds[i]} -')
# shape will print number of rows which indirectly
  means the number
print('Messages Sent', req_df.shape[0])
#Total Messages will yield words per message
Words_per_message = (np.sum(req_df['Word_Count']))/
  req_df.shape[0]

Stats of +91 93754 74744 -
Messages Sent 7
Words per message 8.571428571428571
Stats of +91 80961 54510-
Messages Sent 8
Words per message 6.875
Stats of +91 98485 56739-
```

```
Messages Sent 37
Words per message 20.81081081081081
Stats of +91 95427 58153-
Messages Sent 1
Words per message 19.0
```

10.2 PROGRAM 2: BREAST CANCER PREDICTION

Step 1: Import all the required libraries and modules.

```
import pandas as pd
import numpy as np
import sklearn
```

Step 2: Uploading the data set.

```
from sklearn.datasets import load_breast_cancer
dataset = load_breast_cancer()
```

Step 3: Processing the data and explores the data.

```
dt = pd.DataFrame.from_dict(dataset["data"])
dt.columns = dataset["feature_names"]
dt["target"] = dataset["target"]
```

Step 4: Split the data set as the train and test data sets. Here we considered 70% for training set and 30% as testing set.

```
## Train Test Split
from sklearn.model_selection import train_test_split
X = dt.drop('target', axis=1)
y = dt['target']
X_train, X_test, y_train, y_test = train_test_split(X,
  y, test_size=0.3, random_state=0)
```

Step 5: Import all the required libraries and modules to perform the classification and perform the measures.

```
from sklearn.neighbors import KNeighborsClassifier
from sklearn.metrics import accuracy_score
```

```
from sklearn.model_selection import cross_val_score
import matplotlib.pyplot as plt
%matplotlib inline
```

Step 6: The method k_acc_plot () peforms the classification and calulates the accuracy.

```
## cross-validation accuracy plot with various k
  values
def k_acc_plot(start: int, end: int, X_t, y_t, method:
  str):
## Set k range and initialize lists
k_range = range(start, end)
k_scores = []
train_acc = []
for k in k_range:
knn = KNeighborsClassifier(n_neighbors=k)
knn.fit(X_t, y_t)
accuracy = accuracy_score(y_t, knn.predict(X_t))
scores = cross_val_score(knn, X_t, y_t, cv=5,
  scoring='accuracy')
k_scores.append(scores.mean())
train_acc.append(accuracy.mean())
```

Step 7: Plots the accuracy.

```
## Plot mean CV accuracies for k
plt.title('Mean Training and CV Accuracies vs. k
  after ' + method)
plt.plot(k_range, k_scores, label="CV Accuracy") plt.
  plot(k_range, train_acc, label="Training Accuracy")
  plt.legend()
plt.xlabel('Value of k for kNN')
plt.ylabel('Mean Accuracy')
plt.show()
```

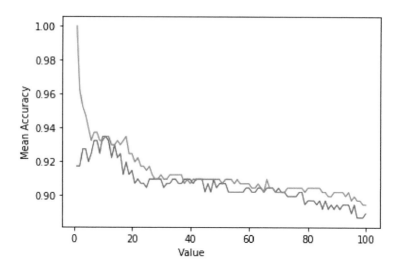

Step 8: Calling the k_acc_plot () to perform the classification.

```
## plot accuracies vs. K values
k_acc_plot(1, 101, X_train, Y_train, "Initial Split")
```

10.3 PROGRAM 3: STOCK PRICE PREDICTION

The stock price prediction involves analyzing the future profitability based on the current environment and the finance. This program deals with identifying the trends in the stock market.

Step 1: Import all the required libraries and modules.

```
import numpy as np
import scipy as sp
import pandas as pd
from subprocess import check_output
import time, json
from datetime import date
import time
import math
import sklearn.preprocessing as prep
import matplotlib.pylab as plt
%matplotlib inline
from matplotlib.pylab import rcParams
```

Step 2: Loading the data set.

```
df= pd.read_csv('stock.csv')
df4=df.set_index("Code")
```

Step 3: Retreiving the unique values of the column code.

```
uniqueVals = df["code"].unique()
```

Step 4: Process the data and calulate the mean of the data.

```
grouped_df=pd.DataFrame()
for i in uniqueVals:
df5 = (df4.loc[i,:]).groupby(['Code','Date']).mean()
# store DataFrame in list
  grouped_df=grouped_df.append(df5)
grouped_df.reset_index()
del df5
```

Step 5: Process the data

```
df1=grouped_df.loc["8KMILES",:]
df2=df1.reset_index()
label=df2['Date'].values.tolist()
trainset=df2['Open'].values.tolist()
df2
```

Step 6: Import all the required libraries and modules to perform.

```
from sklearn.preprocessing import
  StandardScaler,MinMaxScaler
from sklearn.ensemble import RandomForestRegressor
from sklearn.metrics import
  r2_score,mean_squared_error
```

Step 7: Create_dataset() splits the data set.

```
def create_dataset(dataset,past=1):
dataX, dataY = [], []
for i in range(len(dataset)-past-1):
j = dataset[i:(i+past), 0]
dataX.append(j)
dataY.append(dataset[i + past, 0])
```

Step 8: Test and train () transforms the data set.

```
from sklearn.preprocessing import MinMaxScaler
def testandtrain(prices):
scaler = MinMaxScaler(feature_range=(0, 1))
prices = scaler.fit_transform(prices)
trainsize = int(len(prices) * 0.80)
testsize = len(prices) - trainsize
train, test = prices[0:trainsize,:], prices[trainsize
  : len(prices),:]
print(len(train), len(test))
```

Step 9: Performing the train test split and then tranforms the data by calling the methods create_dataset () and test and train ().

```
x_train,y_train = create_dataset(train,1)
x_test,y_test = create_dataset(test,1)
x_train = scaler.fit_transform(x_train)
x_test = scaler.fit_transform(x_test)
#y_test =scaler.fit_transfonm(y_test)
#y_train=scaler.fit_transfonm(y_train)
return x_train,y_train, x_test,y_test
```

Step 10: The close repesents the final price for the stock trades on a specific day.

```
prices = df2['Close'].values.astype('float32')
# Obtaining the values of closing data each day
prices = prices.reshape(len(prices), 1)
prices.shape
```

Step 11: Calling the testandtrain () to transform the data.

```
trainX, trainY, testX, testY=testandtrain(prices)
randomforest = RandomForestRegessor(random_
  state=2017,verbose,n_jobs=5)
randomforest.fit(trainX, trainY)
test=[]
test= randomforest.predict(trainX)
```

Step 12: Plotting the data.

```
plt.plot(test, color="blue")
plt.plot(testY, color='red')
plt.show()
```

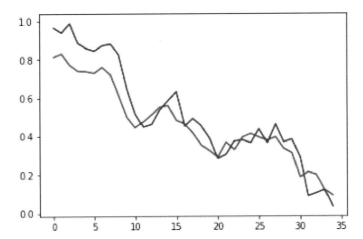

10.4 PROGRAM 4: CHAT BOX

A purpose of the chat box is to communicate an instant message to client.

Step 1: Import all the required libraries and modules.

```
from chatterbot import ChatBot
```

Step 2: Initialization

```
bot = ChatBot(
'usha',
Logic_adapters=[
'chatterbot.logic.BestMatch',
'chatterbot.logic.TimeLogicAdapter'],
)
```

Step 3: Import the libraries

```
From chatterbot. trainers import
  ChatterBotCorpusTrainer
```

Step 4: Process the data

```
trainer = ChatterBotCorpusTrainer(bot)
```

Step 5: Training the data

```
trainer. train('chatterBot.corpus.english')
```

Step 6: Input and displaying the data

```
name=input("Enter Your Name: ")
print("Hi "+name+", May I help you?")
while True:
request=input(name+':')
if request=='Bye' or request =='bye':
print('Usha: Bye')
break
else:
response=bot.get_response(request)
# get_responses() is a method of chatbot instance
print('Usha:', response)
Enter Your Name: usha
Hi usha,how can I help you?
```

10.5 PROGRAM 5: PARKINSON DETECTION

Parkinson is a central nervous system disorder affecting the neurons in the brain.

Step 1: Import all the required libraries and modules.

```
import numpy as np
import pandas as pd
import os, sys
from sklearn.preprocessing import MinMaxScaler
from xgboost import XGBClassifier
from sklearn.model_selection import train_test_split
from sklearn.metrics import accuracy_score
```

Step 2: Reading the data into the data frame.

```
df=pd.read_csv('parkinsons.csv')
df.head()
```

Step 3: Obtain all the features and labels from the data frame. Retrieve all features except the status feature.

```
features=df.loc[:,df.columns!='status'].values[:,1:]
labels=df.loc[:,'status'].values
```

Step 4: Normalizes the features and then transforms by scaling to a specific range. The fit_transforms data transforms the data.

```
scaler=MinMaxScaler((-1,1))
X=scaler.fit_transform(features)
Y=labels
```

Step 5: Split the data set. The test data size is taken as the 20%.

```
x_train,x_test,y_train,y_test=train_test_split(x, y,
  test_size=0.2, random_state=7)
```

Step 6: Train the data set using the XGBoost classifier.

```
model=XGBClassifier()
model.fit(x_train,y_train)
```

Step 7: Generate the predictions and calculate the accuracy.

```
Y_pred=model.predict(x_test)
Print(accuracy_score(y_test, y_pred)*100)
```

94.8717

10.6 PROGRAM 6: FACE MASK

Step 1: Import all the required libraries and modules.

```
from keras.optimizers import RMSprop
from keras.preprocessing.image import
  ImageDataGenerator
import cv2
from keras.models import Sequential
from keras.layers import Conv2D, Input
from keras.layers import ZeroPadding2D,
  BatchNormalization
from keras.layers import Activation, MaxPooling2D
```

```
from keras.layers importFlatten, Dense,Dropout
from keras.models import Model, load_model
from keras.callbacks import TensorBoard,
  ModelCheckpoint
from sklearn.model_Selection import train_test_split
from sklearn.metrics import f1_score
from sklearn.utils import shuffle
import imutils
import numpy as np
```

Step 2: Conv2D is the convolution layer. MAxPooling2D is the max pooling layer. These two layes are used to extract the features from the image that is taken as input. Flaten layer converts the 2D data to the 1D data and drop out takes care of overfitting. The dense layers are used for classification.

```
model = Sequential([
Conv2D(100, (3,3), activation='relu', input_
  shape=(150, 150, 3)),
MaxPooling2D(2,2),
Conv2D(100, (3,3), activation='relu'),
MaxPooling2D(2,2),
Flatten(),
Dropout(0.5),
Dense(50, activation='relu'),
Dense(2, activation='softmax')
])
model.compile(optimizer='adam', loss='binary_
  crossentropy', metrics=['acc'])
```

Step 3: Performed the augmentation uisng the Image Data Generator.

```
train_datagen = ImageDataGenerator(rescale=1.0/255,
rotation_range=40,
width_shift_range=0.2,
height_shift_range=0.2,
shear_range=0.2,
zoom_range=0.2,
horizontal_flip=True,
fill_mode='nearest')
train_generator = train_datagen.flow_from_directory(/
  training,
```

```
batch_size=10,
target_size=(150, 150))
validation_datagen = ImageDataGenerator(resc
  ale=1.0/255) validation_generator = validation_
  datagen.flow/from_directory(/testing,
batch_size-10,
target_size-(150, 150))
```

Step 4: Train the model.

```
history = model.fit_generator(train_generator,
epochs=10,
validation_data=validation_generator,
callbacks=[checkpoint])
```

10.7 PROGRAM 7: COVID-19 ANALYSIS

Step 1: Import all the required libraries and modules.

```
import numpy as np
import pandas as pd
import io
import requests
import matplotlib.pyplot as plt
```

Step 2: Read the data from the specified file.

```
url="covid.csv"
s=requests.get(url).content
```

Step 3: Read the data into the pandas data frame.

```
df = pd.read_csv(io.StringIO(s.decode('utf-8')))
```

Step 4: Converts the data into the datetime format.

```
df['date'] = pd.to_datetime(df['date'],
  format='%y%m%d')
```

Step 5: Removes the unnecessary features from the data set.

```
df.drop(['dateChecked'],axis=1,inplace=True)
```

Step 6: Converts the data feature to the string data type.

```
df['state']=df['state'].apply(str)
```

Step 7: Replacing the NAN values with – 1.

```
df.fillna(value=-1, inplace=True)
```

Step 8: Plotting the hospitalized data.

```
plot_xy('hospitalized','death','IN')
```

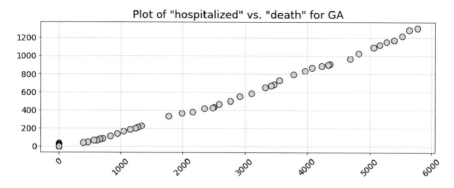

Step 9: Plotting the test positive chart.

```
states = ['CA',NY','MI','MA','PA','IL']
tp,x =[],[]
for s in states:
data = positiveTest_ratio(s)
if data!=-1:
tp.append(data)
x.append(s)
plt.figure(figsize=(8,4))
pit.title("Test-positive ratio chart",fontsize=18)
  plt.xticks(fontsize=14)
plt.yticks(fontsize=14)
plt.bar(x=x,height=tp,color='blue',
edgecolor='k',linewidth=2)
plt.show()
```

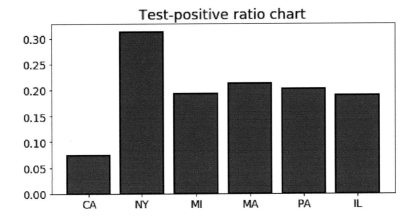

Test-positive ratio chart

10.8 PROGRAM 8: TIME SERIES FORECASTING

To forecast the future and to determine the long-term trend, we use the time series forecasting.

Step 1: Import all the required libraries and modules.

```
import pickle
import warnings
from math import sqrt
import lightgbm as lgb
import matplotlib as mpl
import numpy as np
import pandas as pd
import tensorflow as tf
import xgboost as xgb
from matplotlib import pyplot as plt
from sklearn.metrics import make_scorer, mean_squared_
  error from sklearn.preprocessing import
  StandardScaler
from utils.metrics import evaluate
```

Step 2: Initialization

```
seed = 42
tf.random.set_seed(seed)
np.random.seed(seed)
plt.style.use('bmh')
mpl.rcParams['axes.labelsize'] = 14
mpl.rcParams['xtick.labelsize'] = 12
```

```
mpl.rcParams['ytick.labelsize'] = 12
mpl.rcParams['text.color'] = 'k'
mpl.rcParams['figure.figsize'] = 18, 8
```

Step 3: Reading the data and then parse the data set.

```
d = pd.read_csv('data.csv', parse_dates=['date'])
d.set_index('date', inplace=True)
```

Step 4: Splitting the data set to evaluate the model.

```
# We split our dataset to be able to evaluate our
  models

resultsDict = {}
predictionsDict = {}

d = pd.read_csv('data.csv', parse_dates=['date'])
  d.set_index('date', inplace-True)

split_date = '2021-01-01'
df_training = d.loc[d.index <= split_date]

df_test = dn.loc[d.index > split_date]
print(f"{len(df_training)} days of training data \n
  {len(df_test)} days of testing data ")
```

Step 5: Converting the train and test data to the CSV form.

```
df_training.to_csv('datasets/training.csv')
df_test.to_csv('datasets/test.csv')
```

Step 6: Perform the mean of the data and then evaluate the model.

```
# Also add the naive mean average value
mean = df_training.pollution_today.mean()
mean = np.array([mean for u in range(len(df_test))])
resultsDict['Naive mean'] = evaluate(df_test.
  pollution_today, mean)
predictionsDict['Naive mean'] = mean
resultsDict['Yesterdays value'] = evaluate(
df_test.pollution_today, df_test.pollution_yesterday)
  predictionsDict['Yesterdays value'] = df_test.
  pollution_yesterday.values
```

Step 7: Evalute the model using the XGBoost.

```
reg = xgb.XGBRegressor(objective='reg:squarederror',
  n_estimators=1000)
reg.fit(X_train, y_train,
verbose-False) # Change verbose to True if you want to
  see it train
yhat = reg.predict(X_test)
resultsDict['XGBoost'] = evaluate(df_test.pollution_
  today, yhat)
predictionsDict['XGBoost'] = yhat
```

Step 8: Plotting the time series.

```
plt.plot(df_test.pollution_today.values,
  label='Original')
plt.plot(yhat, color='red', label='XGboost')
plt.legend()
```

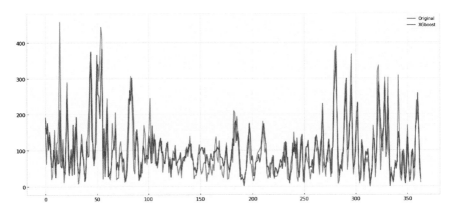

10.9 PROGRAM 9: FRAUD DETECTION

To detect online frauds to prevent financial loss.

Step 1: Import all the required libraries and modules.

```
import pandas as pd
from sklearn.ensemble import RandomForestClassifier
from keras.models import Sequential
from keras.layers import Dense, Dropout, Flatten,
  Activation
from sklearn.metrics import roc_curve
from sklearn.metrics import auc
```

```
import matplotlib as mpl
import matplotlib.pyplot as plt
```

Step 2: Setting the size of the figures.

```
#configure plot size and colors
mpl.rcParams['figure.figsize'] = (10, 10)
colors = plt.rcParams['axes.prop_cycle'].by_key()
  ['color'].
```

Step 3: Read the data and then drop the nan values from the features of the data set.

```
#load data
df = pd.read_csv('frauddata.csv')
#drop NULL values
df = df.dropna()
#drop Time column (contains limited useful
  information)
df = df.drop('Time', axis = 1)
```

Step 4: Each transaction is marked as either fraud or not fraud.

```
#group data by Class
groups = df.groupby('Class')
fraud = (groups.get_group(1).shape[0] / df.shape[0]) *
  100
non_fraud = (groups.get_group(0).shape[0] /
  df.shape[0]) * 100
#print class percentage
print('Percent Fraud: ' + str(fraud) + '%')
print('Percent Not Fraud ' + str(non_fraud) + '%')
```

Step 5: Transform the data on the test data to prevent over biasing.

```
df_size = df.shape[0]
test_size = int(df_size * .3)
train_size = df_size - test_size
train_df = df.head(train_size)
test_df = df.tail(test_size)
X_train = train_df.drop('Class', axis = 1)
Y_train = train_df['Class']
X_train = train_df.drop('Class', axis = 1)
Y_train = test_df['Class']
```

Step 6: Transforming the data set.

```
for feat in X_train.columns.values:
ss = StandardScaler()
x_train[feat] = ss.fit_transform(X_train[feat].values.
  reshape(-1,1))
x_test[feat] = ss.transform(X_test[feat].values.
  reshape(-1,1))
```

Step 7: Fitting the data using the RandomForest model and later find the prediction probabilities.

```
#create Random Forest Model
rf = RandomForestClassifier()
#fit to training data
rf.fit(X_train, Y_train)
#get class probabilities
probabilities = clf.predict_proba(X_test)
y_pred_rf = probabilities[:,1]
```

Step 8: Plotting the ROC graph.

```
plt.plot(100*fpr_rf, 100*tpr_rf, label=
  'Random Forest (area = {:.3f})'.format(auc_rf),
  linewidth=2, color = colors[0])
plt.xlabel('False positives [%]')
plt.ylabel('True positives [%]')
plt.xlim([0,30])
plt.ylim([60,100])
plt.grid(True)
ax = plt.gca()
ax.set_aspect('equal')
plt.title('Random Forest Model Performance') plt.
  legend(loc='best')
```

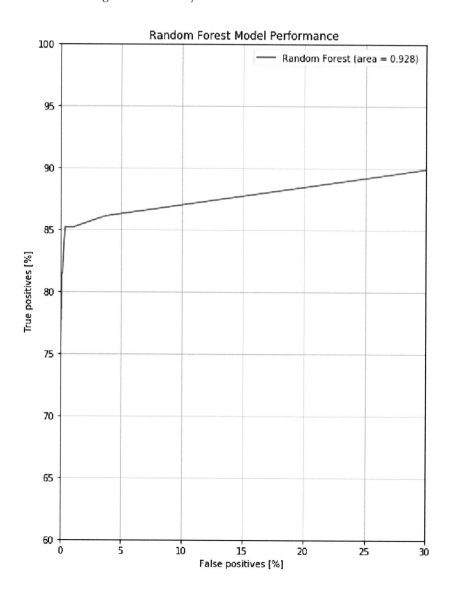

Index